Schizophrenia

Other books by Thomas Szasz

PAIN AND PLEASURE
(1957)

THE MYTH OF MENTAL ILLNESS
(1961)

LAW, LIBERTY, AND PSYCHIATRY
(1963)

PSYCHIATRIC JUSTICE
(1965)

THE ETHICS OF PSYCHOANALYSIS
(1965)

THE MANUFACTURE OF MADNESS
(1970)

IDEOLOGY AND INSANITY
(1970)

THE AGE OF MADNESS (ED.)
(1973)

THE SECOND SIN
(1973)

CEREMONIAL CHEMISTRY
(1974)

HERESIES
(1976)

KARL KRAUS AND THE SOUL-DOCTORS
(1976)

Schizophrenia

The Sacred Symbol
of Psychiatry

THOMAS SZASZ

Basic Books, Inc., Publishers

NEW YORK

The author gratefully acknowledges permission to quote passages from two works by Eugen Bleuler: *Dementia Praecox or the Group of Schizophrenics,* copyright © 1950 by International Universities Press, and *Autistic Undisciplined Thinking in Medicine and How to Overcome It,* reprinted with permission of Macmillan Publishing Co., Inc., copyright © 1969 by Hafner Publishing Co.

Library of Congress Cataloging in Publication Data

Szasz, Thomas Stephen, 1920–
    Schizophrenia: the sacred symbol of psychiatry.

    Includes index.
    1. Schizophrenia. I. Title.
[DNLM: 1. Schizophrenia. WM203 S997s]
RC514.S93   616.8'982   76–27251

TO

Monique Manin-Burke

The legitimate powers of government extend to such acts only as are injurious to others. But it does me no injury for my neighbor to say there are twenty gods, or no God. It neither picks my pocket nor breaks my leg. . . . Constraint . . . may fix him obstinately in his errors, but will not cure them.

Thomas Jefferson (1781)*

* From Thomas Jefferson, "Notes on the State of Virginia," in *The Life and Selected Writings of Thomas Jefferson,* ed. Adrienne Koch and William Peden (New York: Modern Library, 1944), p. 275.

Contents

Acknowledgments

IN THE FALL of 1974 I received an invitation to address the Seventy-second Annual Meeting of the Japanese Society of Psychiatry and Neurology. The main topic of the meeting, scheduled to be held in Tokyo in May 1975, was to be "What Is Schizophrenia?"

This invitation, and the pleasant prospect of also speaking at the University of Kyoto, gave me an impetus to return to and rethink my contributions to this subject dating back twenty years,[1] and to restate, in a systematic way, my views on what —in both psychiatry and anti-psychiatry—now passes under the heading of schizophrenia. Soon I found myself putting on paper many more words than I could possibly deliver at a lecture. The result is this book. The occasional references in it to Japanese psychiatry—which I would not otherwise have made, but which there seemed no reason to delete—are thus attributable to this circumstance.

I wish to take this opportunity to thank, once more, my hosts in Japan, particularly Dr. Tadao Miyamoto, President of the Seventy-second Annual Meeting of the Japanese Society of Psychiatry and Neurology; Dr. Tomio Hirai, President of the Japanese Society of Psychiatry and Neurology; Dr. Kiyoshi Ogura of Tokyo; Dr. Hiroshi Ohashi, Professor of Psychiatry and Neurology at Kyoto University; Dr. Kotaro Nakayama of Kyoto; and Dr. Kenji Sakamoto of Osaka. I am grateful to them not only for inviting me to Japan, but also for making my visit personally enjoyable and professionally rewarding.

I wish to thank also George Szasz, my brother; Margot Szasz Peters and Susan Marie Szasz, my daughters; Ronald Carino,

Acknowledgments

Joseph DeVeaugh-Geiss, Jonathan Ecker, and Kathleen McNamara, my friends and colleagues; Paul Neuthaler, my editor at Basic Books; and Debbie Murphy, my secretary. They have all been generous and sympathetic with their help in making this book possible.

Preface

EVERY GROUP or organization whose members are held together by shared ideas and ideals has its distinguishing symbols and rituals. For Christians the most sacred symbol is the cross and the most revered ritual is the Mass; for physicians they are the M.D. degree and the diagnosis of disease.

Persons, both as individuals and as group members, experience such symbols and rituals as their most treasured possessions which they must zealously protect from usurpation by others, especially nonmembers. In effect, they regard them as holy things whose purity they must vigilantly safeguard against pollution by insiders and outsiders alike.

Psychiatrists constitute a group. Since they are physicians, their guild is a subgroup of the medical profession as a whole. The two groups thus share, as their major symbol and ritual, the M.D. degree and the diagnosis of disease. They also share many of the other symbols and rituals of medicine, such as the white coat, the prescription blank, and the use of hospitals, clinics, nurses, and drugs. If these are the symbols and rituals that regular physicians and psychiatrists share, which are the symbols and rituals that distinguish them?

The symbol that most specifically characterizes psychiatrists as members of a distinct group of doctors is the concept of schizophrenia; and the ritual that does so most clearly is their diagnosing this disease in persons who do not want to be their patients.

When a priest blesses water, it turns into holy water—and thus becomes the carrier of the most beneficent powers. Similarly, when a psychiatrist curses a person, he turns into a schizophrenic—and thus becomes the carrier of the most maleficent powers. Like "divine" and "demonic," "schizophrenic" is a concept wonderfully vague in its content and terrifyingly awesome in its implications.

In this book I shall try to show how schizophrenia has become the Christ on the cross that psychiatrists worship, and in whose name they march in the battle to reconquer reason from unreason, sanity from insanity; how reverence toward it has become the mark of psychiatric orthodoxy, and irreverence toward it the mark of psychiatric heresy; and how our understanding of both psychiatry and schizophrenia may be advanced by approaching this "diagnosis" as if it pointed to a religious symbol rather than to a medical disease.

Chapter 1

Psychiatry: The Model of the Syphilitic Mind

WHAT IS SCHIZOPHRENIA? What does the term *schizophrenia* mean? In its most elementary sense, we might say that schizophrenia is a word—an idea and a "disease"—invented by Eugen Bleuler, just as psychoanalysis is a word—an idea and a "treatment"—invented by Sigmund Freud, and Coca-Cola is a name—an idea and a soft drink—invented by whoever invented it.* The point I wish to emphasize here, right at the outset, is that the claim that some people have a disease called schizophrenia (and that some, presumably, do not) was based not on any medical discovery but only on medical authority; that it was, in other words, the result not of empirical or scientific work, but of ethical and political decision making.[2] To appreciate the nature and import of this distinction we shall have to review, briefly but carefully, our concept of disease, especially as it existed in the context of the medical culture in which Bleuler announced his invention.

Let us try to project ourselves back into the minds of physicians and psychiatrists in, say, 1900. When they spoke of disease, what did they mean? They meant, typically, something like

* Actually, the beverage, originally containing a mixture of cocaine and an extract of the kola nut, was invented in 1886 by John S. Pemberton. Its name was invented by Pemberton's friend and bookkeeper, Frank M. Robinson.[1] "Coca-Cola" and "Coke" are today the

syphilis. "Know syphilis in all its manifestations and relations," declared Sir William Osler (1849–1919), "and all things clinical will be added unto you." [3] This is obviously no longer true today. Indeed, how many cases of syphilis do modern medical students see? In the United States, Osler's maxim has been replaced by another which asserts that "Mental illness is our number one health problem." This would make schizophrenia— the most common and most disabling of the so-called mental diseases—the successor to Osler's syphilis, showing us immediately what a gulf separates us from him. For, clearly, a physician may know all there is to know about schizophrenia and still be totally ignorant of medicine.

The Oslerian image thus points to a lesson we forget at our own peril. That lesson is the agreement among modern physicians as scientists—tacit but nonetheless total—that they will do their utmost to distinguish between complaints and lesions, between being a patient and having a disease; and their resolution to regard as diseases only those processes occurring in the body (human or animal) which they can identify, measure, and demonstrate in an objective, physicochemical manner. This was one of the reasons why syphilis was the turn-of-the-century medical paradigm of disease. Another was that it was common. And a third was that the syphilitic infection could affect countless organs and tissues, causing discrete lesions which could be appropriately named, all of which were, nevertheless, a part of the general systemic disease called syphilis. Thanks to the work of numerous medical investigators around the turn of the century, physicians finally grasped that such totally dissimilar biological phenomena as the genital chancre of primary syphilis, the dermatitis of secondary syphilis, and the general paraly-

---

most imitated and most litigated trademarks. In view of the fact that neither "schizophrenia" nor "psychoanalysis" could be, or were ever, registered as trademarks, psychiatrists and psychoanalysts have been amazingly successful in cornering and controlling the market for these "products."

sis of the insane of tertiary syphilis were actually all different manifestations of the same disease process, called syphilis.

What made these monumental medical discoveries important, besides the prophylactic and therapeutic benefits for which they were essential, was that they paved the way toward establishing the empirical and epistemological criteria for judging whether or not a person had syphilis. In other words, with the development of clear-cut anatomical, histological, biochemical, immunological, and clinical criteria for syphilis, it was possible to establish, with a great deal of accuracy, not only that certain persons hitherto unsuspected of this disease were in fact syphilitics, but that others, suspected of it, were not.

These developments were of the most far-reaching importance for physicians, including psychiatrists, working at that time. By about 1900 European psychiatry was a well-established medical specialty. Its respectability, both scientifically and politically, depended wholly on the medical perspective—perhaps we ought to say medical premise—that the psychiatrist's patients, like those of the regular physician or surgeon, suffered from diseases. The difference, in this view, between non-psychiatric patients and psychiatric patients was that whereas the diseases of the former caused them to have fevers and pains, those of the latter caused them to have hallucinations and delusions. Thus, to Theodor Meynert (1833–1892), Freud's professor at the University of Vienna Medical School, it was clear that disease meant anatomical abnormality, and accordingly he searched for and postulated such abnormalities to account for all so-called mental diseases. His "vasomotor theory," writes Zilboorg, "combined with a systematized outline of what each part of the central nervous system does or fails to do in mental diseases, permitted Meynert to offer a classification of mental diseases on a purely anatomical basis." [4] Meynert sought to reduce psychiatry to neurology and, quite reasonably and revealingly, he objected not only to psychological explanations of so-called psychiatric illnesses but even to the term *psychiatry* itself.

5

The discovery of the syphilitic origin of paresis was a brilliant scientific confirmation of this organic-psychiatric hypothesis—namely, that persons whose brains are abnormal are likely to exhibit behavior commonly judged abnormal. With paresis as its paradigm, psychiatry became the diagnosis, study, and treatment of "mental diseases"—that is, of abnormal biological processes within the patient's head manifested by the psychological and social "symptoms" of his illness. Psychiatry—whether organic or not, as Freud and his followers have subscribed to this model as slavishly as their organic opponents [5]—thus became fatefully tied to medicine and its core concepts of illness and treatment. It is necessary that we understand exactly how this happened.

There are experiences that we may read about, and know about intellectually, but cannot, without living through them personally, appreciate in their full human impact. Most people who are well cannot, in this sense, grasp what it is to be desperately ill; those who are rich, what it is to be desperately poor.

In the same way, people cannot now grasp the impact which neurosyphilis exerted on institutional psychiatry during the crucial first four decades of its existence—that is, between 1900 and 1940. Most psychiatrists now practicing in the major industrial societies never see a patient with neurosyphilis. Many physicians have never seen one in their whole lives. For medical students, the disease has already become almost as legendary—in the sense of esoteric and extinct—as leprosy had been generations ago.

It is against this contemporary background that we must re-inspect the frequency and reconsider the role of neurosyphilis during the formative decades of modern psychiatry. Until the advent of penicillin in the 1940s, a large proportion of patients admitted to mental institutions throughout the world suffered from general paresis. Here are some illustrative figures. In the mental hospital Dalldorf in Berlin, from 22 to 32 percent of the patients admitted between 1892 and 1902 had paresis. At the Central State Hospital in Indianapolis, Indiana, between 1927 and 1931, from 20 to 25 percent of the newly admitted patients were paretics. At the Tokyo Insane Hospital in 1930, 30 percent of the patients admitted were paretics.[6] And so it went throughout the world.

Is it any wonder, then, that paresis was deeply imprinted into the mind and memory of psychiatry? And that psychiatry still speaks with the accents of neurosyphilis on its lips? To vary the metaphor, it is as if paresis had been a traumatic event, or indeed a series of such events, in the childhood of psychiatry. Now, while asleep, psychiatry still dreams about it; while awake, it sees the world as if the specter of paresis lurked behind every foolish face or troubled thought. Thus has the image of the crooked spirochete making people mad been replaced, in the minds of many psychiatrists, by the image of the crooked molecule making them mad.

Viewed against the historical background I have sketched, the story of the origin of the modern concepts of dementia praecox and schizophrenia appears, to me at least, in quite a different light from that in which it is usually presented.

The officially accepted form of this story is, briefly, that in the second half of the nineteenth century, medical scientists began to be able to identify the precise morphological character and material causes of many diseases, and that this led quickly to effective methods of prevention, treatment, and cure for some of these diseases. For example, physicians learned to identify many of the infectious diseases and their causes: puerperal fever, tuberculosis, syphilis, gonorrhea, scarlet fever, and so on; they also learned how to prevent and treat some of them.

According to this version of the history of psychiatry, as some medical investigators discovered and identified diphtheria, so others—in particular Kraepelin—discovered and identified dementia praecox; as some discovered and identified syphilis, so others—in particular, Bleuler—discovered and identified schizophrenia.

As I see it, this is not what happened at all. It is true that around the turn of the last century, medical investigators discovered and identified a host of diseases—in particular, the major infectious diseases of that age. But it is not true that psychiatric investigators discovered and identified certain other diseases—in particular, dementia praecox, schizophrenia, or other so-called functional psychoses (or neuroses). Psychiatrists made no discoveries according to which the people allegedly suffering from these diseases would have qualified by Virchow's criteria—and there were no others at that time—as having a disease.

It cannot be emphasized enough in this connection that until Rudolph Virchow's (1821–1902) great work, *Die Cellularpathologie* (1858), the concept of disease was abstract and theoretical, rather than concrete and empirical; and that it became abstract and theoretical again with the introduction of psychopathological, psychoanalytic, psychosomatic, and psychodynamic concepts and terms into nosology.

Before Virchow, the model of disease was "humoral pathology"; since him, it has been "cellular pathology." More precisely, until about 1800 diseases were supposed to be due to an imbalance of the four fluid humors of the body—that is, blood, phlegm, yellow bile, and black bile. This concept dated back as far as the Greeks. In 1761 Giovanni Morgagni, an Italian anatomist, showed that diseases were due not to an imbalance of humors but to lesions in organs. Around 1800 Xavier Bichat, a French anatomist, demonstrated that the human body was composed of twenty-one different kinds of tissues, and suggested that only some of the tissues in a diseased organ might be affected. It was, however, not until 1858, when Virchow delivered his famous twenty lectures, published as *Die Cellular-pathologie in ihrer Begründung auf physiologische und pathologische Gewerbelehre* (*Cellular Pathology Based on Physiological and Pathological Histology*), that the model of disease as cellular pathology was firmly established.[7] According to this view, "Disease of the body is a disease of cells. The cure of the body may be effected by curing the cells. The real question which the modern scientific physician puts to himself when called to treat a case is: What cells are out of order and what can be done for them?" [8] This remains the basic concept and model of disease in Western countries and in scientific discourse throughout the world.

It must be noted, therefore, that Kraepelin and Bleuler discovered no histopathological lesions or pathophysiological processes in their patients. Instead, they acted *as if* they had discovered such lesions or processes; named their "patients" accordingly; and committed themselves and their followers to the goal of establishing a precise identification of the "organic" nature and cause of these diseases. In other words, Kraepelin and Bleuler did not discover the diseases for which they are famous; they invented them.*

Because of the dominating role and importance of schizophrenia in modern psychiatry, it is easy to fall into the trap of believing that schizophrenia has always been an important problem in this field, and in the world. This is simply not so.

---

* It is important to note here that psychiatrists have looked to paresis as the paradigm not only of the psychoses but of the neuroses as well. In 1925 Freud reiterated his belief that "the true spontaneous neuroses resembled no group of diseases more closely than the phenomena of intoxication and abstinence, which are produced by the administration or privation of certain toxic substances. . . ." [9] This view, he says,

Actually, the concept of dementia praecox, as we now know it, was invented by Emil Kraepelin (1855–1926) in 1898. He has since been hailed as a great medical scientist, as if he had discovered a new disease or developed a new treatment; in fact, he did neither. What he did, according to Arieti—who is very respectful toward his achievement—was this: "Kraepelin's insight consisted in including three conditions under one syndrome." [11] The three "conditions" were "catatonia," or stupors, originally described by Karl Ludwig Kahlbaum (1828–1899); "hebephrenia," or silly and stilted behavior, partially described by Ewald Hecker (1843–1909); and "vesania typica," or hallucinations and delusions, also previously described by Kahlbaum. The point I want to emphasize here is that each of these terms refers to behavior, not disease; to disapproved conduct, not histopathological change; hence, they may loosely be called "conditions," but they are not, strictly speaking, medical conditions. If none of these three items is a disease, putting them together still does not add up to a disease. Nevertheless, the unpleasantness of the persons who displayed such "psychotic" behavior, the actual or seeming social incapacity of the "patients," and the professional prestige of physicians such as Kraepelin sufficed to establish dementia praecox as a disease whose histopathology, etiology, and treatment now awaited only the further advances of medical science.

Without waiting for such developments to occur, the disease

"pleased" his "medical conscience" because by having arrived at it "I hoped that I had filled up a gap in medical science, which, in dealing with a function of such great biological importance, had failed to take into account any injuries beyond those caused by infection or by gross anatomical lesions." [10]

As these two sentences—and, indeed, the whole of his work—show, Freud never ceased flirting with the aim of extending the paradigm of paresis from "injuries . . . caused by infection or by gross anatomical lesions" to "injuries" caused by as yet unidentified toxic chemicals. In short, both the neuroses and psychoses were, in his view, "organic" diseases.

was etymologically enhanced. Its name was changed from Latin to Greek—that is, from dementia praecox to schizophrenia. And its incidence—that is, its epidemiological significance—was increased with the stroke of a pen. All this was done by Eugen Bleuler (1857–1939) who, again according to Arieti,

> accepted the fundamental nosologic concept of Kraepelin but enlarged it to a great extent, because he considered as related to dementia praecox many other conditions such as psychosis with psychopathic personalities, alcoholic hallucinoses, etc. Furthermore, he thought that the largest number of patients are never hospitalized because their symptoms are not severe enough; that is, they are latent cases.[12]

The imagery and vocabulary of syphilology are unmistakable here: "severe cases" requiring confinement, and "latent cases" lurking about without the patient realizing that he is ill. (According to Freud, homosexuality and virtually every other kind of "psychopathology" could also be either overt or latent.) Since Bleuler, too, neither discovered a new disease nor developed a new treatment, his fame rests, in my opinion, on having invented a new disease—and, through it, a new justification for regarding the psychiatrist as a physician, the schizophrenic as a patient, and the prison where the former confines the latter as a hospital.

Still, the question remained: Just what was schizophrenia? Eugen Bleuler answered this question—at least to the satisfaction of most psychiatrists, past and present.

Prior to 1900 psychiatrists believed that paresis was due to bad heredity, alcoholism, smoking, and masturbation. These beliefs are now of only historical interest, like the belief in demonic possession or exorcism. We celebrate and credit with discoveries the physicians—Alzheimer, Schaudinn, Wassermann, Noguchi, and Moore—whose work demonstrated irrefutably that paresis was due to, and was a manifestation of, syphilis.

Similarly, today psychiatrists believe that schizophrenia is due to, and is a manifestation of, an organic disease of the brain. Batchelor's phrasing is illustrative: "Both Kraepelin and Bleuler believed that schizophrenia was the outcome of a pathological, anatomical, or chemical disturbance of the brain." [13] But why should we care about what Kraepelin and Bleuler *believed?* Bleuler also believed in abstaining from alcohol and in the metaphoric rather than literal interpretation of the Eucharist. These beliefs of Bleuler's are of no more consequence for the histopathology of schizophrenia than are Fleming's religious beliefs for the therapeutic powers of penicillin. Why, then, do psychiatrists continue to record Kraepelin's and Bleuler's *beliefs* regarding the nature of schizophrenia? Why do they not emphasize instead Kraepelin's and Bleuler's utter inability to support their beliefs with a shred of relevant *evidence?*

Actually, Kraepelin and Bleuler were psychiatric clinicians, not medical investigators. Hence, they were not in a favorable position to generate any truly relevant evidence in support of their beliefs regarding the etiology or pathology of schizophrenia. Instead, what they did was subtly to redefine the criterion of disease, from histopathology to psychopathology—that is, from abnormal bodily structure to abnormal personal behavior. Since it was unquestionably true that most people confined in mental hospitals "misbehaved," this opened the road toward charting the maps of psychopathology, thus identifying "existing" mental diseases and "discovering" new ones. It will repay us to review exactly how Bleuler achieved this scientific sleight of hand. The following quotations are from Bleuler's *Dementia Praecox or the Group of Schizophrenias,* published in 1911:

> By the term "dementia praecox" or "schizophrenia" we designate a group of psychoses whose course is at times

chronic, at times marked by intermittent attacks, and which can stop or retrograde at any stage, but does not permit a full restitutio ad integrum. The disease is characterized by a specific type of alteration of thinking. . . .[14]

But "alteration of thinking" is irrelevant from a strictly medical or physicochemical point of view. The fact that paresis is a brain disease could never have been established by studying the paretic's thinking. Then why study the schizophrenic's? Not, it seems to me, in order to prove that he is sick: that has already been established by the *presumption* of psychiatric authority whose power neither patient nor laymen can match, and which no colleague dare challenge. The schizophrenic's thinking is thus anatomized and pathologized in order to create a science of psychopathology, and then of psychoanalysis and psycho-dynamics, all of which in turn serve to legitimize the madman as a medical (psychiatric) patient, and the mad-doctor as a medical (psychiatric) healer.

Throughout his book Bleuler emphasizes that the schizophrenic patient suffers from a "thinking disorder" manifested by a "language disorder." His book is full of illustrations of the remarks, pleas, letters, and other linguistic productions of so-called schizophrenic patients.[15] He offers many comments about language, of which the following is typical:

Blocking, poverty of ideas, incoherence, clouding, delusions, and emotional anomalies are expressed in the language of the patients. However, the abnormality does not lie in the language itself, but rather in its content.[16]

Here, and elsewhere, Bleuler goes to great effort to protect himself against creating the impression that in describing a schizophrenic patient he is merely describing someone who speaks oddly or differently than he does, and with whom he,

Bleuler, disagrees. He never ceases to emphasize that this is not the case, that, on the contrary, the "patient" is sick and his linguistic behavior is only a "symptom" of his "illness." Here is one of Bleuler's statements epitomizing this line of argument:

> The form of linguistic expression may show every imaginable abnormality, or be absolutely correct. We often find very convincing ways of speaking in intelligent individuals. At times, I was unable to convince all of my audiences attending clinical demonstrations of the pathology of such severely schizophrenic logic.[17]

Bleuler's premise and posture here preclude—and seem intended to preclude—questioning that the so-called schizophrenic is "sick," that he is a bona fide "patient." We are allowed to question only in what way he is sick—what sort of illness he has, what sort of "pathology" his "thinking" exhibits. To assent to this is, of course, to give away the game before beginning to play it.

Actually, often the only thing "wrong" (as it were) with the so-called schizophrenic is that he speaks in metaphors unacceptable to his audience, in particular to his psychiatrist. Sometimes Bleuler comes close to acknowledging this. For example, he writes that

> a patient says that he is being "subjected to rape," although his confinement in a mental hospital constitutes a different kind of violation of his person. To a large extent, *inappropriate figures of speech* are employed, particularly the word "murder," which recurs constantly for all forms of torment and in the most varied combinations (italics added).[18]

Here, I submit, we have a rare opportunity to see how language displays what is quintessentially human, and, at the same time, to see how language may be used to deprive individuals of their humanity. When persons imprisoned in mental hospitals speak of "rape" and "murder," they use inappropriate figures of speech which signify that they suffer from thought disorders; when psychiatrists call their prisons "hospitals," their prisoners "patients," and their "patients' " desire for liberty "disease," the psychiatrists are not using figures of speech, but are stating facts.

The remarkable thing about all of this is that Bleuler understood perfectly well, probably much better than do many psychiatrists today, that much of what appears strange or objectionable in schizophrenic language is the way such persons use metaphor. Nevertheless, he felt justified, on the ground of this fact alone—as the following vignette illustrates—in regarding such persons as suffering from a disease in the literal rather than metaphorical sense:

> When one patient declares that she is Switzerland, or when another wants to take a bunch of flowers to bed with her so that she will not awaken any more—these utterances seem to be quite incomprehensible at first glance. But we obtain a key to the explanation by virtue of the knowledge that these patients readily substitute similarities for identities and think in symbols infinitely more frequently than the healthy: that is, they employ symbols without any regard for their appropriateness in the given situation.[19]

Bleuler's explanation of these "symptoms" creates still further problems for the psychiatrist, logician, and civil libertarian. For this now-classic psychiatric perspective presses these questions upon us: If what makes "schizophrenic" utterances "symptoms" is that they are incomprehensible, do they still remain "symptoms" after they are no longer incomprehensible? If the utterances are comprehensible, why confine those who utter them in madhouses? Indeed, why confine persons even if their utterances are incomprehensible? These are the questions Bleuler never asks. Moreover, these questions cannot be raised in psychiatry even today, for such queries expose the empires of psychiatry as being as devoid of visible diseases as the legendary emperor was of visible clothes.

Consider in this connection the woman patient who, Bleuler writes, " 'possesses' Switzerland; and in the same sense she says, 'I am Switzerland.' She may also say, 'I am freedom,' since for her Switzerland meant nothing else than freedom." [20] What makes this woman a "schizophrenic" rather than a "poet"? Bleuler explains:

The difference between the use of such phrases in the healthy and in the schizophrenics rests in the fact that in the former it is a mere metaphor whereas for the patients the dividing line between direct and indirect representation has been obscured. The result is that they frequently think of these metaphors in a literal sense.[21]

The source of Bleuler's egocentric and ethnocentric fallacy is dramatically evident here. Would a Catholic psychiatrist writing in a Catholic country have expressed himself so cavalierly about the literalization of metaphor constituting the cardinal symptom of schizophrenia, the most malignant form of madness known to medical science? For what, from a Protestant point of view, is the Catholic doctrine of transubstantiation if not the literalization of a metaphor? [22] *Mutatis mutandis,* I hold that the psychiatric conception of mental illness is also a literalized metaphor. The main difference, in my view, between these cardinal Catholic and psychiatric metaphors and the metaphors of so-called schizophrenic patients lies not in any linguistic or logical peculiarity of the symbols but in their social legitimacy—the former being legitimate metaphors and the latter being illegitimate.

Thus, slowly and subtly but surely indeed, Bleuler—and, of course, Freud, Jung, and the other pioneer psychopathologists and psychoanalysts—managed to bring about the great epistemological transformation of our medical age: from histopathology to psychopathology. It is now unappreciated how closely these three men worked together in the crucial few years before the outbreak of World War I, and how intimately intertwined were the earliest developments of psychoanalysis and psychopathology. The first psychoanalytic journal, published in 1909, was entitled *Jahrbuch für Psychoanalytische und Psychopathologische Forschungen* (*Yearbook for Psychoanalytic and Psychopathologic Investigations*). Its publishers were Eugen Bleuler and Sigmund Freud, and its editor was Carl Jung. Bleuler was then the professor of psychiatry, and Jung a Privatdozent, at the University of Zürich Medical School.[23]

Freud's fondness for pathologizing psychology—that is, life itself—was, of course, fully disclosed eight years earlier, in his popular work *The Psychopathology of Everyday Life* (1901).[24] It was in this book that he most fully developed "his belief in the universal application of determinism to mental events." [25] Concepts such as "idea," "choice," and "decision" all become, in Freud's hands, "events," and all are "determined." "I believe," he writes, "in external (real) chance, it is true, but not in internal (psychical) accidental events." [26] Thus have Bleuler, Freud, and their followers transformed our image and idea of illness, and our vocabulary for describing and defining it; thus have they displaced lesion by language, disease by disagreement, pathophysiology by psychohistory—and, generally, histopathology by psychopathology.

Although modern psychiatry began with the study of paresis and the efforts to cure it, it soon turned into the study of psychopathology and the efforts to control it. Psychiatry thus replaced what had formerly been known as mad-doctoring, psychiatrists henceforth playing the roles of mad-doctors—that is, controlling not diseases but deviants. Through this pseudoscientific transformation of the alienist into the psychiatrist, psychiatry became—and is now everywhere accepted as—the "scientific" study of misbehavior and its "medical" management. And schizophrenia is its sacred symbol—the largest grab bag of all the misbehaviors which psychiatrists, coerced by society or convinced by their own zeal, are now ready to diagnose, prognose, and therapize. This ceremonial role of schizophrenia in psychiatry is illustrated by the publication, and the contents, of the recent *International Pilot Study of Schizophrenia,* [27] conducted under the auspices of the World Health Organization (WHO).

The authors of this study list the following four characteristics —they call them "inclusion criteria"—which, when observed about, or attributed to, a person by a psychiatrist, qualify that person as a schizophrenic: "(1) Delusions. (2) Definitely inappropriate or unusual behavior. (3) Hallucinations. (4) Gross psychomotor disorder; over- and under-activity. . . . Inclusion criteria 1–4 automatically qualified the patient for inclusion, regardless of the severity of the symptomatology." [28]

The briefest critical scrutiny of this list makes its scientific and medical pretensions vanish—like the frightened child's ghost being dispelled by flicking on the light in the bedroom.

Delusions. We know what they are: believing that you are one of the Chosen People; or that Jesus is the son of God who died, but has been resurrected and is now still alive; or that Freud was a scientist and psychoanalysis is a science of the unconscious mind; or that gold will always be worth $35 (U.S.) an ounce.

Inappropriate or unusual behavior. Well, we know that, too, when we see it: attacking Pearl Harbor, or invading Vietnam; having long hair or short hair or no hair; setting yourself on fire, committing hara-kiri, or jumping off the Golden Gate Bridge.

Hallucinations. No problem here, either: communicating with deities or dead people (and being unsuccessful at claiming a "divine calling" or being a spiritualist); or seeing one's childhood or other long-past events (in one's mind's eye) and relating them to someone who insists that the speaker "actually" sees them.

Over- and under-activity. This hits close to home: the eighteen- to twenty-hour working day of a busy American doctor; the porch sitting and television watching of a healthy but forcibly retired American worker. Or closer still: traveling halfway across the world to attend a psychiatric meeting and falling asleep while listening to the presentation of the papers.

I hope I will be forgiven my levity. I am using it, at this point, deliberately to dramatize the degree to which psychiatry has been debauched by persons who prefer to be policemen rather than physicians.

Let us not forget that medicine had been pregnant with psychiatry for a long time—for almost 250 years, from the middle of the seventeenth century, when it was impregnated by the founding of madhouses, until the end of the nineteenth century and the beginning of the twentieth, when Kraepelin and Bleuler gave birth to the living medical specialty of psychiatry. This birth was duly celebrated by a christening. The baby's last name was a double one, as befits a noble offspring: medicine, from the mother, and psychiatry, from the father. Hence the specialty of "psychiatric medicine." In addition, the child had to be identified by given names as well: these were bestowed upon it by its two great accoucheurs, Kraepelin and Bleuler, to whom we owe the names "dementia praecox" and "schizophrenia." Their authoritative legitimization of all sorts of medically healthy persons as sick—that is, as mentally sick—was the crucial event signifying the birth of modern psychiatry. This, briefly, is how it all happened.

When Kraepelin, Bleuler, and their contemporaries became psychiatrists, psychiatry was already an established form of medical and medicolegal practice. Moreover, the real locus of that practice was the insane asylum or mental hospital, just as the real locus of the surgeon's practice was the operating room. What distinguished an important, successful psychiatrist from his less important psychiatric colleagues and from his colleagues in other medical specialties was that he was the director or superintendent of an insane asylum or mental hospital. This meant that he had the authority, at once medical and legal, to keep innocent men and women—often thousands of them— under lock and key.

In addition, the medical and social definitions of madness being what they were (and still are), the majority of the patients brought to the attention of men like Kraepelin and Bleuler were considered to be mentally ill before, often long before, they reached these psychiatrists. The upshot was that these men reigned over hospitals full of people who were regarded—by their relatives, by other physicians, by the law—as bona fide patients. The pressure—both scientific and social—on these men was therefore all one way: define the madman as sick and discover in what way or for what reason he is sick!

Still, could these institutional psychiatrists have not taken a more independent, more scientifically honest position? Could they have not told themselves that, as medical scientists, one of their foremost duties was to ascertain what was and what was not a disease? To discover which persons complaining or suspected of disease were and were not sick? And could they have not acted accordingly?

Had those physicians taken such a position, they could have asked themselves further whether, in fact, it was not their first duty toward the inmates of their hospitals to examine them medically; and to declare, on the basis of their examination, whether or not they found them to be suffering from an illness? Actually, given the Virchowian criteria of disease and the social facts of psychiatry which then prevailed, I do not believe that Kraepelin, Bleuler, or the other psychiatrists of that period could have assumed such a role, and gotten away with it. The reason is simple. They would have had to conclude that most of the "patients" in their hospitals were not sick; at least, they could not have found anything demonstrably wrong with the anatomical structure or physiological functioning of their bodies. But this would have undermined the justification for the patients' confinement, which, after all—and everyone knew this, even if no one was willing to admit it—was the real reason these people were called "patients" and were "hospitalized" in the first place.*

It is, in fact, overwhelmingly clear that institutional psychiatrists could not, at that time, have declared their "patients" as "medically well" and survived as professionals, as physicians and psychiatrists. Indeed, they still cannot do so. The "patients' " relatives, physicians, and society in general wanted to segregate certain disturbing persons, and had done so in mad-

---

* In his psychiatric "confessions," about which I shall have more to say presently, Bleuler refers to the pressures to diagnose madmen as genuinely sick under which he and his colleagues worked: "Almost as difficult as saying 'I can't give any help,' or 'I don't know,' or at any rate much too hard for a great number of doctors, is the statement 'I find nothing wrong,' when he makes an examination of the patient. When a doctor feels duty-bound to find *something,* yet without sufficient grounds or evidence, and only to please the patient or himself, a ticklish problem is posed." [29] Not quite: a ticklish problem is not so much posed as it is bypassed, and ticklish new problems—that is, new "diseases," new "medical" interventions, and new complications caused by such interventions—are created.

A few pages later Bleuler returns to this subject, remarking: "Similarly we allow ourselves to be oriented and 'slanted' by other family members and acquaintances in our clinical as well as in our institutional practice." [30]

houses. This was a *fait accompli*—on a massive scale, at that—by the time Kraepelin and Bleuler arrived on the psychiatric scene. Had they said that their so-called patients (or many of them) were not sick, they would have cut the ground from under the accepted justification for confinement. The medical profession, the psychiatric profession, the legal profession, and society as a whole would not have stood for it. They would have gotten rid of such psychiatrists and replaced them with men who did what was expected of them. And they would have richly rewarded those who so fulfilled society's needs for social control and scapegoating—as indeed they have rewarded Kraepelin, Bleuler, and their loyal and mindless followers.

This, in brief, is why I consider Kraepelin, Bleuler, and Freud the conquistadors and colonizers of the mind of man. Society, their society, wanted them to extend the boundaries of medicine over morals and law—and they did so; it wanted them to extend the boundaries of illness from the body to behavior—and they did so; it wanted them to disguise conflict as psychopathology, and confinement as psychiatric therapy—and they did so.*

I have argued that in isolating schizophrenia, Bleuler did not identify "just another" disease, such as diabetes or diphtheria, but justified the established practice of confining madmen by compulsory hospitalization. Bleuler was aware of this. In his monograph on schizophrenia he remarks: "Once the disease

---

* As I noted in passing, Kraepelin, Bleuler, and Freud were not the first such conquistadors and colonizers. The process I describe began during the Enlightenment and its true pioneers were the late-eighteenth-century alienists.[31] However, these early inventors of "medical insanity" stand in the same relation to Kraepelin, Bleuler, and Freud—who made ours the age of "mental illness"—as the inventors of the internal combustion engine stand to Henry Ford and the other industrial and merchandising geniuses who made ours also the age of the automobile.

has been recognized, the question as to whether or not to institutionalize the patient must be decided." [32] By whom? Clearly, Bleuler does not mean that it is to be decided by the patient! Hence, from the point of view of the "patient" who does not want to be confined in a mental hospital, the so-called "recognition of the disease" is obviously a harmful rather than a helpful act. Much of this, too, Bleuler acknowledges:

> The institution as such does not cure the disease. However, it may be valuable from an educational viewpoint and it may alleviate acute, agitated states due to psychic influences. At the same time, it carries with it the danger that the patient may become too estranged from normal life, and also that the relatives get accustomed to the idea of the institution. For this reason, it is often extremely difficult to place even a greatly improved patient outside the institution, after he has been hospitalized for a number of years.[33]

In other words, the function of the involuntary hospitalization of the "schizophrenic" is to relieve his relatives of the burden which he is to them. Realizing all this, Bleuler was caught in the grips of a moral dilemma he could not satisfactorily resolve. Like American jurists before the Civil War who disapproved morally of slavery but felt bound by the Constitution to uphold it as the law, Bleuler, too, was caught between the demands of justice and the dictates of necessity.[34] Justice demanded that people diagnosed as schizophrenic be treated, like other patients, as free and responsible citizens. Necessity dictated that "schizophrenics," like convicted criminals, be deprived of their liberty. The upshot was that while Bleuler preached freedom for schizophrenics, he practiced psychiatric slavery and legitimized it by means of an elaborate pseudomedical "theory" concerning the "disease" that transforms free citizens into psychiatric slaves (that is, schizophrenic patients).[35]

Bleuler knew perfectly well that, in actuality, the diagnosis of schizophrenia functioned and was used as a justification for compulsory hospitalization—just as, in another context, the "diagnosis" of blackness functioned and was used as a justification for slavery. Nevertheless, he pleads that it "should not" be so used: "The patient should not be admitted to the hospital just because he suffers from schizophrenia, but only when there is a definite indication for hospitalization." [36] But insofar as the "patient" diagnosed as schizophrenic is deprived of his right to self-determination, it is pointless to preach this counsel of psychiatric moderation. For if commitment for schizophrenia is a legal option, what countervailing force is there to stop relatives, social institutions, and psychiatrists from confining any or all persons diagnosed as schizophrenic? There is none, and Bleuler knew it. Still he plunges on, defining his own criteria of the "correct" indications for committing schizophrenics:

> The indication is, of course, given when the patient becomes too disturbing or dangerous, when restraint is necessary, when he presents a threat to the well-being of the healthy members of his family, or when it is no longer possible to influence him. In the latter event, the institution will attempt to educate the patient to act in a more acceptable manner, after which he will be released.[37]

The unruly child is ordered to stand in the corner, after which he is allowed to rejoin his classmates. A graver indictment of involuntary mental hospitalization as a fake medical intervention—as a procedure for punishing and "educating" the misbehaving child-"patient"—would be difficult to find, or even to imagine. Ironically, in a footnote to this discussion Bleuler castigates "bad, overcrowded institutions" in which schizophrenics are turned into "work-slaves by the hospital personnel who treat them as if they were merely obstinate, healthy persons." [38]

Until the Civil War, many Americans could not clearly confront the essential moral problem of involuntary servitude—namely: What, if anything, justifies slavery? Similarly, Bleuler and most of his contemporaries could not, and most people today still cannot, clearly confront the essential moral problem of institutional psychiatry—namely: What, if anything, justifies involuntary mental hospitalization and other compulsory psychiatric interventions? This is why even men like Jefferson extolled freedom and practiced slavery, and why even men like Bleuler extolled psychiatric toleration but practiced psychiatric tyranny.

Astonishingly, my foregoing assumptions and assertions find support in Bleuler's original text on schizophrenia. Most of this support, moreover, is packed into the very last paragraph of this long book. Here, in Bleuler's own words, is his recognition of two of my crucial contentions—namely, that the institutional psychiatrist is not the patient's agent but society's, and that many of his interventions are not treatments but tortures:

The most serious of all schizophrenic symptoms is the suicidal drive. I am even taking this opportunity to state clearly that our present-day social system demands great and entirely inappropriate cruelty from the psychiatrist in this respect. People are being forced to continue a life that has become unbearable for them for valid reasons; this alone is bad enough. However, it is even worse, when life is made increasingly intolerable for these patients by using every means to subject them to constant humiliating surveillance.[39]

This is a very honest, but also self-incriminating, admission on Bleuler's part. For he acknowledges here not only that the psychiatrist acts as society's agent vis-à-vis the involuntary mental patient, but also that what society demands of its psychiatrist-agent is "cruelty"! This seems to me exceedingly similar to recognizing that, say, in a society given to brutal methods of executions, executioners are expected by the state to torture their victims; or that, in a totalitarian society, judges are expected by the state to preside over trials in which innocent persons are systematically sentenced to harsh punishments. Execrable as all such arrangements are, it is important to remember that in each of them the victimizer is, more or less, a free agent. The state, even a totalitarian state, does not force individuals to be brutal executioners, or corrupt judges, or institutional psychiatrists. Individuals accept or assume these roles voluntarily or willingly—in exchange for the goods and services, the prestige and power, which society bestows on them for doing its dirty work. Bleuler acknowledges all this:

> Most of our worst restraining devices would be unnecessary if we were not duty-bound to preserve the patients' lives which, for them as well as for others, are only of negative value. If all this would, at least, serve some purpose! . . . I am convinced that in schizophrenia it is this very surveillance which awakes, increases, and maintains the suicidal drive. Only in exceptional cases would any of our patients commit suicide, if they were permitted to do as they wished. And even if a few more killed themselves—does this reason justify the fact that we torture hundreds of patients and aggravate their disease? At the present time, we psychiatrists are burdened with the tragic responsibility of obeying the cruel views of society; but it is our responsibility to do our utmost to bring about a change in these views in the near future.[40]

I do not doubt Bleuler's sincerity. But it is a sincerity whose moral force is blunted by its being self-serving. Bleuler must have known that no one—especially in Switzerland—is forced to be cruel to anyone else. He must have known, too, that to attribute all of the cruelty with which madmen are treated to society—and, again, to an exceptionally civilized and decent Swiss society—is disingenuous. The result—so patently selfserving—of Bleuler's foregoing explanation for psychiatric barbarities is to imply that psychiatrists in general, and he in particular, are not to blame for them. On the contrary, they are all trying to improve the system!

Alas, if it had only been true. The better part of the twentieth century has elapsed since Bleuler wrote the above lines. This was a period of the most momentous technological changes and social transformations. The only thing that has remained virtually unchanged is involuntary psychiatry: mental patients, especially if they are "dangerous to themselves or others," are still confined, just as they were in 1911; their confinement is still rationalized as "treatment," just as it was then; and they are brutalized and tortured (though the methods by which this is accomplished have changed), much as they were then.

Nor could it have been otherwise so long as no prestigious individual or group spoke out, or assumed a responsible position, in opposition to involuntary psychiatry. Bleuler and his colleagues practiced involuntary psychiatry, and by so doing authenticated the very practices which Bleuler denounces. Acts speak louder than words. Psychiatrists could not remedy the moral wrongs Bleuler has pointed to so long as they themselves participated in committing them. And they still cannot do so. It is not enough to murmur that psychiatric coercion is bad; it is necessary systematically to condemn it and eschew it. That is the simple, but inescapable, lesson which the history of institutional psychiatry teaches us.

Further confirmation of my foregoing thesis may be found in a most unexpected source. In 1919, when Bleuler was sixty-two years old and his reputation as an asylum psychiatrist second to none in the world, he wrote a little book that is, in effect, an attack on asylum psychiatry. This book, oddly titled *Autistic*

Undisciplined Thinking in Medicine and How to Overcome It,
is very little known.[41] It is never referred to in psychiatric circles. And for good reasons, as I shall now try to show.

In a preface to *Autistic Thinking*—the title alluding, of
course, to autism, one of the cardinal "Bleulerian" symptoms of
schizophrenia—Manfred Bleuler, the author's son and himself
a prominent institutional psychiatrist, observes that when his
father wrote this book he was "known only for his publications
dealing with psychopathological problems. . . . [Nevertheless,]
he had the audacity to write a biting, even downright crude
criticism of medical practice and medical science in simple,
earthy, and at times peasant-like words." [42] Most of Bleuler's
criticism in this book is actually directed not against medicine
but against psychiatry—or against both, insofar as Bleuler often
made no sharp distinction between medical and psychiatric
practice. It is important to reemphasize that Bleuler wrote this
book in plain—"earthy . . . peasant-like"—language. Why
this sharp departure from writing in bombastic medical jargon,
by the very person who coined some of our key psychiatric
terms, including "autism" and "schizophrenia"? I submit that it
is an indication that Bleuler recognized that the use of pseudomedical terminology in psychiatry is itself unscientific and immoral. But it is time to let Bleuler—the confessor, not the
conquistador—speak for himself. Trying to debunk the notion
that a person is ill merely because he or she is taking a "cure,"
he relates this episode:

> I do not recall the details, but I hope I can give you the
> main gist of the matter. The lady told me, "My daughter
> spent last winter on the Riviera and took a cure there. Then
> she went to Baden-Baden to the sanatorium of Dr. N.," (and
> then on to some other famous place—name, witness
> knoweth not), "and now she is drinking the waters at St.
> Moritz and taking the fresh air cure in the Engadine."
>
> "What is your daughter suffering from?" I asked.

"Oh, yes, she's got to recuperate."

"From what?" I asked again.

"Yes, she's just got to recuperate."

No different from this is the situation in respect to scores of other medical prescriptions enjoining rest cure. . . . The whole question of recovery has nothing to do with recreation, and the idleness in a sanatorium can do more harm than good.[43]

A few lines down the same page, Bleuler offers a vignette illustrating clearly what "schizophrenia" is really all about. It is a far cry from his earlier picture of it as a "mental disease":

A young girl, recently discharged [from a sanatorium], is somewhat delicate and also "nervous," so the doctor forbids her to accept employment or to learn anything useful to give meaning to her life. What can she do? She cannot in good conscience get married. So she is *condemned to make her illness her lifetime career,* in other words, vegetate and decay in idleness. . . . Since woman can without working gain a living with relative ease, such advice as this is extremely dangerous. *It is still an open question, and a very important one, whether women really have a greater tendency to nervous diseases, or whether the opportunities for leading a parasitic existence constitute the real reason for their greater neurotic morbidity** (italics in original).[44]

In this book, Bleuler actually goes so far as to acknowledge that the concept of mental illness, especially as it is used in institutional psychiatry, is not a medical concept at all:

Certain aspects of the concept of disease have of course been discussed often enough . . . and modern legislation compels

* I consider the connections between matrimony and psychiatry, personal incapacity and psychiatric invalidity, in Chapter 4.

us to make a clear though perhaps fragmentary definition here and there. But definitions of this type are forensic and not medical.[45]

These remarks, with which I agree, are wholly inconsistent with Bleuler's treatise on schizophrenia and with his textbook of psychiatry, both of which are devoted to identifying and defining "mental illnesses" as medical, not forensic, concepts and entities!

Halfway into this book we find Bleuler comparing doctors to schizophrenics—because each believes things for which there is no evidence, and because each is fond of covering up his ignorance with flowery language:

> We administer all sorts of treatments whose efficacy has never been proved, such as electricity; or treatments about which we are insufficiently informed, such as water in hydrotherapy. . . . There is always the exaggerated impulse to "do something" to combat an illness, in place of calm reflection. . . . We observe this urge to glibness among small children, among savages, among doctors, and in tales from mythology; also to some extent in the discourse of philosophers; and in morbid form, among schizophrenics, in particular. . . . It is upon this primal urge that the power of medical practice is founded.[46]

As he warms to his subject, Bleuler alternately, or even in the same sentence, ridicules medical jargon and redeploys it:

> When the doctor wishes to give the patient a modicum of encouragement he tells him that his state of nerves is due to overwork; if he wishes to give himself a boost and puff up his ego at the patient's expense, he tells him that his nervous condition is due to masturbation; both statements are au-

tistic. . . . Careless thinking is oligophrenic and leads to error; autistic thinking is paranoid and leads to hallucination.[47]

Despite his attempts to cut through the maze of medical jargon and to be sincere rather than "scientific," Bleuler succumbs here to his habit, by now deeply ingrained, of pathologizing behavior. Thus, behavior that is simply stupid, selfserving, exploitative, or vicious, he calls "oligophrenic" and "autistic." Perhaps it is the specter of syphilis hovering in the background that makes him still think of (mis)behavior as disease, as the following deeply revealing sentences suggest:

Is it right to shoot Salvarsan into the veins of every patient whose Wassermann Test is positive? Many a case of "latent" schizophrenia is diagnosed as total in all certainty. Never does it occur to the doctor to consider all the consequences: confinement of the patient to a mental institution, deprivation of civil rights, abandonment of his profession, etc.[48]

Clearly, this little book is not only Bleuler's attack on psychiatry; it is also a confessional of his own sins. For it was Bleuler, after all, who—through his book on schizophrenia, his textbook on psychiatry, and his own work as an asylum psychiatrist—articulated, authenticated, and advocated the principles and practices of involuntary psychiatry, which he here scathingly criticizes.

Once Bleuler assumes the posture of psychiatric critic, he soon recognizes that, in his society, much passes for illness that is nothing of the sort. "But is it really necessary," he asks rhetorically, "always to speak of neurasthenia, that disease resulting from strain and overwork, when the true cause of the illness is on the contrary a timid fear of the real tasks of life, and figuratively speaking, a slap in the face would be the best remedy for some lazy whining patient worrying about his health?" [49]

But it is not ideas and books such as these that made Eugen Bleuler the director of the Burghölzli and professor of psychiatry at the University of Zürich. Manfred Bleuler, who rose to assume the same positions his father had held, repudiates his father's heresy almost as if the roles were reversed —he being the father scolding his son for his "irresponsibility":

> This venture placed his career in the balance. Warnings of friends were by no means lacking. . . . Reviewers . . . condemned him for undermining the dignity and ethical standards of the medical profession. Many persons advised the author to refrain from such escapades in the future, to stick to his last and preserve his loyalty to his own technical field.[50]

Nowhere does Manfred Bleuler say that he thinks, or that others had thought, that what his father wrote in this little book was not true. Instead, he talks about Eugen Bleuler's "escapade," of his "disloyalty" to his own profession, and, above all else, of his "irresponsibility." "At the first clinical lecture I attended as a young student," Manfred Bleuler reminisces, "a famous teacher, frowning with disapproval, spoke of the irresponsibility with which the author undermined all the standard, tried and true methods of medical therapy." [51]

These words, written in 1969, faithfully reflect the official party line of organized psychiatry. The Bleuler of 1911—the conqueror of schizophrenia *for* psychiatry—is venerated as a veritable saint. The Bleuler of 1919—the protector of the "patient" *from* a conquering psychiatry—is patronized by his son and ignored by his profession.

Modern psychiatry—who would disagree?—is a powerful ideology and institution. On what sacred symbols and ritual ceremonies does it rest? I have tried to show in my work during the past twenty years that it rests on the imagery and vocabulary of mental illness, hospitalization, and treatment. What, then, would happen to psychiatry if medicine and law, people and politicians, recognized the metaphoric and mythological character of mental illness? Such demythologizing of psychiatry would undermine and destroy psychiatry as a medical specialty just as surely as the demythologizing of the Eucharist would undermine and destroy Roman Catholicism as a religion. To be sure, there would remain the behavior or misbehavior of the so-called schizophrenic and of the psychiatrist, but their behavior would constitute problems for ethics and politics, semantics and sociology—not jurisdictions for control by medicine and psychiatry. Similarly, there would remain, after the demythologizing of the Eucharist, the moral problems of persons and the moral prescriptions of priests, but all these, too, would be problems for ethics and politics—not jurisdictions for control by Church and pope.*

* The literalization of the metaphor of the Eucharist demanded by the doctrine of transubstantiation is not accepted by all modern Catholic theologians. According to one authoritative source, "The Eucharist is the actualizing of the salvific reality of 'Jesus,' through the words of thanksgiving uttered over bread and wine. . . . It was only the spirituality of the Hellenistic community which linked the presence of Christ materially to the element of the meal. . . . The real presence of Jesus in the consecrated elements as thus conceived, is, therefore, only a Hellenistic interpretation which is today no longer possible." [52]

However, this liberal interpretation of the doctrine of transubstantiation exaggerates the rejection by Roman Catholics of the literal interpretation of the Eucharist. On September 3, 1965, only three years before the above was written, in his encyclical *Mysterium Fidei,* Pope Paul VI "called for a retention of the full reality of the Catholic faith about the Presence of Christ in the Eucharist, and specifically for a retention of the dogma of transubstantiation, together with the received terminology in which it has been expressed, particularly at the Council of Trent." [53]

In any case, I am offering this comparison between theological and psychiatric metaphors to expose and criticize beliefs and practices based on the literalization of the metaphor of mental illness, not to expose or criticize beliefs and practices based on the literalization of the metaphor

It is obvious—to non-Catholics—that the doctrine of transubstantiation is a case of metaphor literalized for certain perfectly valid practical reasons. All non-Catholics, and even many Catholics, recognize that wine and wafer are just that, and not the body and blood of a man long dead who is said to be a deity. In certain situations, however, they all behave, Catholics more often than non-Catholics, as if the symbol were the thing symbolized. The question is: Why do people act this way? Catholics do mainly because this is what establishes their identity as Catholics, an identity they desire to preserve. Non-Catholics do mainly because it is—say, in a church—the polite thing to do.

Similarly, it is equally obvious—to nonpsychiatric physicians —that the belief in mental illness is another case of metaphor literalized for perfecly valid practical reasons. Most nonpsychiatrists, and even many psychiatrists and laymen, recognize that cadavers can have diabetes and syphilis, but cannot have depression and schizophrenia; in other words, that disagreements and misbehaviors are just that, and not the symptoms of undemonstrated and undemonstrable lesions or processes in the dark recesses of the brain. In certain situations, however, they all behave, psychiatrists more often than nonpsychiatrists, as if the symbol were the thing symbolized; that is, as if schizophrenia were actually like syphilis and depression like diabetes. The question is: Why do people act like this? Psychiatrists do mainly because this is what establishes their identity as physicians, an identity they desire to preserve. Nonpsychiatrists—physicians, patients, and laymen alike—do mainly because, as a rule, it is the polite and proper thing to do in our society lest one risk revealing oneself as stupid or sick.

---

of the Eucharist. The success of the latter enterprise is enshrined in the First Amendment to the Constitution of the United States; the failure of the former enterprise, in the psychiatric subversion of the Rule of Law and the psychiatric deprivation of freedoms guaranteed by the Constitution.

The gist of my argument is that men like Kraepelin, Bleuler, and Freud were not what they claimed or seem to be—namely, physicians or medical investigators; they were, in fact, religious-political leaders and conquerors. Instead of discovering new diseases, they extended, through psychiatry, the imagery, vocabulary, jurisdiction, and hence the territory of medicine to what were not, and are not, diseases in the original, Virchowian, sense. Again we may ask: Why did they do this? Why did they not declare, instead, that persons thought to be suffering from schizophrenia (and other functional psychoses or neuroses) could, at least at that stage of medical science, not be shown to have any demonstrable diseases, and that, until they could, they ought to be regarded as not sick? Why, in other words, did they *presume* that the persons entrusted to their care were sick until proven otherwise? Indeed, that there was no "otherwise": that they *were* sick, and it was merely a matter of time until the histopathology of their diseases would be demonstrated?

The answers to these questions are absolutely crucial for a proper understanding of the history of modern psychiatry in general, and of schizophrenia in particular. Furthermore, in answering these questions we come upon a confluence of the two great streams of thought, and of the error in each, which seems to me to be the source of the confusion and crime that constitute much of modern psychiatry: the two streams are epistemology and ethics (or, more narrowly, medicine and law); the two errors are confusing disease with disagreement (body with behavior, objects with agents) and confusing patients with prisoners (cure with control, therapy with torture).

Thus, the problem that faced Kraepelin and Bleuler was, in fact, exquisitely moral and political, economic and existential. I would compare it to the problem that has faced, and continues to face, national leaders and party politicians in countries like Japan and the United States which are confronted with a pressing need for, and a painful shortage of, oil. What should they do? Take the oil by force and supply the necessary national, moral, political, and economic justification for doing so (such as national interest or economic strangulation)? Or should they acknowledge national sovereignty and free trade as principles applicable to the interests of others no less than to their own, and try to accommodate to their situation without the use of force?

Where, it may be objected, is there any parallel or similarity between the present political dilemma over oil, and the dilemma of European psychiatry over madness at the turn of the century? What has psychiatry to do with force, with violence, with conquest? It has, of course, everything to do with them. For what was the so-called "clinical material"—the oil, as it were—with which Kraepelin, Bleuler, and their colleagues in institutional practice worked? If a person were to answer "mental patients," "psychotics," or "schizophrenics," then he would be wrong—as wrong as if he said that Abu Dhabi had launched a military attack on Japan or the United States in 1974. Actually, the so-called clinical material—and this term is itself richly revealing of the martial and indeed colonial strands in the fabric of modern medicine—with which these psychiatrists worked was not patients but prisoners. Some were prisoners in the literal or legal sense; others were prisoners in the sense that they had been apprehended and confined by force, though they had not been sentenced to imprisonment for any crime.

I refer here to some elementary facts and their extremely far-reaching, though systematically denied and confused, consequences. The facts are that, in the main, so-called madmen —the persons whom we now call schizophrenic and psychotic— are not so much disturbed as they are disturbing; it is not so much that they themselves suffer (although they may), but that they make others (especially members of their family) suffer. The consequences of these facts are that, in the main, so-called schizophrenics or psychotics do not regard or define themselves as ill and do not seek medical (or, often, any other kind of) help. Instead, other people—usually members of their family, sometimes their employers, the police, or other authorities—declare and define them as ill and seek and impose "help" on them.

In this connection, it is interesting to consider the traditional Japanese practice of dealing with madmen—the system of the so-called "private imprisonment" of the mentally ill.[54] Under this system, so-called psychotic patients were confined at home. It was a sort of house arrest, such as is still practiced in some countries when highly placed persons are charged with an offense, especially of a political sort. This Japanese practice, which prevailed until the end of World War II, is portrayed by Western observers in absurdly chauvinistic terms; that is, they take it for granted that the systematic brutalization of madmen in European madhouses was more humane than whatever care or neglect Japanese mental patients received at the hands of their own families.[55] This seems to me rather unlikely.

In any case, the point I am making is that in Japan, under the "law of private imprisonment," so-called psychotic persons were confined and "cared" for against their will. In Europe, the United States, and South America, persons of this sort were also managed involuntarily; that is, they themselves did not, as a rule, seek help, but were defined as sick by others and were "hospitalized" and "treated" against their will. Indeed, as recently as when I was a medical student in the early 1940s, the regulations of the state mental hospitals in Ohio excluded admission of voluntary patients. The only way to be admitted to such hospitals was by commitment, which could be medical or judicial. This reflected more closely than do conditions now the real nature of such hospitals and such hospitalization. A person cannot now gain admission to a prison by showing up at the gate and announcing that he is a criminal; similarly, he could not then gain admission to a mental hospital (at least in some jurisdictions) by showing up at the gate and claiming that he was mentally ill. In each case there had to be a legal, or quasi-legal, determination of his eligibility for such confinement. I emphasize this to drive home the point that Kraepelin and Bleuler were not primarily physicians. They were wardens.

The differences between progress in medicine and psychiatry which I have tried to delineate here are so crucial that I want to restate them from a somewhat different angle.

Medical pioneers discover new treatments and formulate new theories of the effects of their treatments to help persons afflicted with certain preexisting bodily afflictions called "diseases." Banting discovered insulin, Minot discovered liver extract, and Fleming discovered penicillin. Because these substances proved useful for patients suffering, respectively, from diabetes, pernicious anemia, and certain infectious diseases, they were defined—by physicians, patients, and people generally—as treatments.

Psychiatric pioneers invent new diseases and formulate new theories of the etiology of these diseases to justify calling certain preexisting social interventions "treatments." Kraepelin invented dementia praecox, and Bleuler schizophrenia, to justify calling psychiatric imprisonment "mental hospitalization" and regarding it as a form of medical treatment; having new diseases on their hands, they attributed them to as yet undetected defects of the brain. Freud invented the neuroses to justify calling conversation and confession "psychoanalysis" and regarding it, too, as a form of medical treatment; having a class of new diseases on his hands, he attributed them to the "vicissitudes of the Oedipus complex." Menninger invented the idea that everyone is mentally ill to justify calling every-thing that anyone did to anyone else, ostensibly with good intentions, "the therapeutic attitude"; having all of life on his hands as a new disease, he attributed it to disturbances in "the vital balance." [56]

Real medicine thus helps real physicians to treat or cure real patients; fake medicine (psychiatry) helps fake physicians (psychiatrists) to influence or control fake patients (the men-tally sick).

Kraepelin and Bleuler were, of course, directly involved in placing the shackles of the law and of the lock on so-called psychotics. Freud's involvement, though less direct, was no less significant: he regarded "psychotics" as deranged and mad, "inaccessible" to psychoanalysis or psychotherapy, lacking "insight" into their "illness," and fit subjects for psychiatric confinement. In his most famous study of schizophrenia, the Schreber case, Freud devotes page after page to speculations about the character and cause of Schreber's "illness," but not a word to the problem posed by his imprisonment or to his right to freedom.[57] Schreber, who was a "psychotic," ques-tioned the legitimacy of his confinement, and Schreber, the madman, sought and secured his freedom. Freud, who was a "psychoanalyst," never questioned the legitimacy of Schreber's confinement, and Freud, the psychopathologist, cared no more about Schreber's freedom than a pathologist cares about the freedom of one of his specimens preserved in alcohol.

Freud's official silence on commitment—not only Schreber's but of mental patients generally—seems to me decisive evi-dence of his view on this matter. After all, he expressed him-self on every other subject in psychiatry, and on countless sub-jects outside of it. The fact that throughout his long life Freud, in his professional writings, completely ignored involuntary psychiatry is eloquent testimony to how very natural and right it must have seemed to him that "psychotics" should be locked up by psychiatrists.* It is obvious, moreover, that as a psychiatric conquistador—as an extender of the frontiers of medicine over morals and all of life itself—Freud was even more ambitious, and more successful, than Kraepelin and Bleuler. It is almost as if these two great institutional psychiatrists had limited their ambitions to medicalizing those who were confined, or deemed fit to be confined, to madhouses. Freud, on the other hand, acknowledged no limits to his thirst for conquest; he considered the whole world his consulting room, and everyone in it a patient whom he had a right to "psychoanalyze," "psychopathologize," and, of course, "diagnose."

Such reflections suggest that the history of modern psychiatry is actually a sort of replay (with appropriate changes in the cast of characters and their deeds to conform to contemporary conditions) of the ancient legend of Ulysses blinding the Cyclops.[61] As may be recalled, the Cyclopes were a tribe of fearful giants with a single eye located in the middle of their foreheads. Ulysses and his crew fell victim to them and were held captive by one of them.

How did Ulysses overcome the Cyclops? He told him that his name was "Nobody" and proceeded to operate on the Cyclops'

* The suspicion that Freud was wholly in favor of locking up recalcitrant mental patients is supported not only by his never having publicly said or professionally written a critical word about this practice, but also by his letter of May 6, 1908, to Jung. It begins as follows: "Dear friend, Enclosed the certificate for Otto Gross. Once you have him, don't let him out before October, when I shall be able to take charge of him." [58] Otto Gross, the "patient" referred to here, was a physician who was then being "treated" by Jung at the Burghölzli hospital for addiction to cocaine and opium. For a while both Freud and Jung regarded Gross as a promising recruit for the psychoanalytic movement. But Gross proved to be too uncooperative, both as a patient and as a psychiatrist. In June 1908 Freud writes to Jung: "Unfortunately there is nothing to be said of him [Gross]. He is addicted and can only do great harm to our cause." [59] Ironically, in October of the same year Gross published a letter in Die Zukunft, a prestigious Berlin periodical, in which he objected to the commitment to a mental hospital of a young woman by her father.[60]

eye. When the Cyclops, shrieking in agony, was asked what was the matter, he replied: "Nobody is blinding me." His fellow Cyclopes concluded that he was crazy, and Ulysses and his men made good their escape.

The credibility of this legend depends on several hidden dramatic and logical devices to which I want to call attention. First, it depends on Ulysses' name: Nobody. Second, it depends on the precise semantic structure of the wounded giant's complaint; that is, on his saying "Nobody is blinding me," instead of, for example, "A man who calls himself Nobody is blinding me." And third, it depends on the other Cyclopes' forming a judgment based only on a report. Had they gone and looked at what was happening, they would have seen the facts for themselves.

When the keepers of madhouses call their prisoners "patients" and their prisoners' (mis)behavior "diseases," and when they call themselves "doctors" and their punishments "treatments," they are, in effect, pulling the same ruse on us (and perhaps even on themselves) as Ulysses pulled on the Cyclops. By attaching the names of illnesses to certain behaviors and the roles of patients to the people who exhibited them, Kraepelin, Bleuler, and Freud laid the ground for the "Nobody is blinding me" sort of deception and self-deception. They named some things in such a way that when subsequently they or others uttered assertions that included these names, people were led to believe that they were hearing about diseases and patients. In fact, they were not being told about diseases or patients; their acceptance of the deception depended on the operation of the same three dramatic and logical devices to which I called attention a moment ago. It will repay us to repeat them and articulate them as they apply to the legends of lunacy.

The first requirement was the appropriate naming of the legendary hero—Ulysses in the old legend, the various forms of lunacy in the new. Giving them the names of diseases in Latin and Greek, and their bearers the names of patients, also in these sacred languages, fulfilled this requirement.

The second requirement was the issuing of appropriate reports about the legendary events—the blinding of the Cyclops in the old one, the manifestations of lunacy and the misdeeds of lunatics in the new one. The so-called clinical descriptions of mental diseases and the so-called histories of mental patients met this requirement.

But all this would not have worked had the third requirement not also been met—that is, if those who listened to these stories had not been willing and eager to form a judgment based solely on the reports they heard. If the nonpsychiatrists—like the Cyclopes of old—had only gone and looked at what was happening, they would have seen the facts for themselves. By facts, I mean quite simply that the Cyclopes would have seen that someone had blinded one of their fellows, and that whoever did it used the name "Nobody" to conceal his deed. Similarly, ordinary men and women could have seen that the psychiatrist treats healthy people as if they were sick patients, imprisons them as if they were convicted offenders, and uses the name "schizophrenia" to conceal his deeds.

Of course, we do not know (and need not ask, as it is, after all, a legend) why the Cyclopes did not check the facts for themselves. On the other hand, we know only too well (and hence need not ask, as the story about schizophrenia is, after all, not a legend) why ordinary men and women did not check the facts for themselves: as the saying has it, no one is so blind as the person who does not want to see. Many people did not want to see in the past, and do not want to see now, the naked facts of psychiatry—namely, that psychiatrists diagnose diseases without lesions, and treat patients without rights.

This, then, was the fateful point of departure in the origin of modern psychiatry: the invention of the alleged disease "schizophrenia"—a disease whose lesion no one could see, and which "afflicted" persons in such a way that often they wanted nothing more than not to be patients. This is not as surprising as it might seem in view of the fact that Kraepelin and Bleuler grew into mature professionals under the shadow of the spirochete. Moreover, they lived to see its conquest, at least diagnostically. Hence, they were impressed not only by paresis as a model of psychosis, but also by latent syphilis—a disease without morphologic lesion (recognizable only through an immunological test of the blood) and without symptoms (and therefore without the motive of suffering prompting the "sick person" to assume the patient role). Thus, it was probably latent syphilis as much as it was paresis that seduced Kraepelin and Bleuler into placing their faith in the model of syphilis as holding the solution for the riddle of "mental disorders." These assumptions are supported by Kraepelin's following remarks, offered in 1917, at the height of his career:

> The nature of most mental disorders is now obscured. But no one will deny that further research will uncover new facts in so young a science as ours; in this respect the diseases produced by syphilis are an object lesson. It is logical to assume that we shall succeed in uncovering the causes of many other types of insanity that can be prevented—perhaps even cured—though at present we have not the slightest clue. . . .[62]

Almost sixty years have elapsed since that statement. And the "new facts" in our "science" are that, although we may have lots of new facts about neurochemistry and psychopharmacology, we have none about schizophrenia. We know neither what it is nor what causes it. Still, we have made progress in understanding its etiology: we no longer believe and claim that schizophrenia is caused by masturbation. And we have made progress in understanding what it is: the WHO *Report,* to which I referred earlier, actually acknowledges that schizophrenia is a *word*. It may require only a few hundred years more of intensive psychiatric and epidemiological research to discover that it is *only* a word.

"Why," ask the authors of this study, "is a concept of schizophrenia necessary at all?" They answer their own question as follows: "Firstly, because we have the term. The word schizophrenia has come into such widespread use that it is necessary to have a practical definition of it in order to keep public discussion of schizophrenia within reasonable limits." [63]

During the past two decades I have devoted much work and many words to exposing the scientific stupidity, the philosophical folly, and the moral monstrosity of this official psychiatric posture, and shall refrain from repeating these arguments here. Perhaps we are now or will soon be ready to look at some "old facts" which have stubbornly stood in the way of so-called psychiatric progress. Among these I would single out, first, the differences between suffering and being sick, personal (mis)behavior and pathophysiological dysfunction, and curing disease and controlling deviance; and second, the moral, political, and legal dimensions of psychiatric practices posing vexing questions concerning the human rights—that is, the civil or legal rights—of so-called mental patients.

I call these "old facts" partly to distinguish them from the "new facts" generated by empirical science, and partly to emphasize that their relevance to the problem of schizophrenia suggests, at least to me, that the solution of this problem may lie not so much in the direction of medical research (though, if done competently and honestly, it may still yield some valuable results) as in the direction of a philosophical, moral, and legal reassessment of what so-called schizophrenics do or fail to do, and what psychiatrists (and lawyers and judges) do for and to them.

Chapter 2

Anti-Psychiatry: The Model of the Plundered Mind

WITH THE RAPID DEVELOPMENTS in syphilology, psychiatry, and psychoanalysis during the first two decades of this century, there occurred a division of the spoils, as it were, among them: paresis was claimed by syphilology, psychosis by psychiatry, and neurosis by psychoanalysis. The result was two reciprocal series of differentiations: patients became separated into paretics, psychotics, and neurotics; doctors, into syphilologists (and neurologists), psychiatrists, and psychoanalysts (and psychotherapists). Separating the patients was, and is still, called making a "differential diagnosis." Separating the physicians was, and is still, called "specializing" in the diagnosis and treatment of one or another branch of medicine.

In keeping with the general character of classifications, each of these categories of patients and doctors had a characteristic member which became its model. The paradigmatic patients displayed the supposedly typical medical diseases of their class, whereas the paradigmatic doctors displayed the supposedly typical medical interventions of theirs: paresis thus became the paradigm of neurosyphilis, schizophrenia of psychosis, and hysteria of neurosis; similarly, chemotherapy (and artificial fever) became the paradigm of syphilology, psychiatric incarceration (called "mental hospitalization") of psychiatry, and conversation (called "free association" and "interpretation") of psychoanalysis.

I emphasize these historical changes—which were partly

caused by certain fresh scientific discoveries which in turn generated some fresh social practices—in order to identify as clearly as possible the nature of "traditional" psychiatry as it existed, say, at the end of World War II. As a sharpshooter must see his target clearly, so we must see psychiatry clearly—for both the so-called anti-psychiatrists and I have aimed our critical firepower at it. As I shall now try to show, we have, however, done so in very different ways, and for very different reasons.

One of the developments since the first publication of *The Myth of Mental Illness,*[1] and attributable in no small part to its influence, is the so-called anti-psychiatry movement. This movement, like the movement of traditional psychiatry which it seeks to supplant, is also centered on the concept of schizophrenia and on helping so-called schizophrenics. Because both the anti-psychiatrists and I oppose certain aspects of psychiatry, our views are often combined and confused, and we are often identified as the common enemies of all of psychiatry.

It is true, of course, that in traditional, coercive psychiatry, the anti-psychiatrists and I face the same enemy. So did, in another context, Stalin and Churchill. The old Arab proverb that "the enemy of my enemy is my friend" makes good sense indeed in politics and war. But it makes no sense at all in intellectual and moral discourse.

I reject the term *anti-psychiatry* because it is imprecise, misleading, and cheaply self-aggrandizing. Chemists do not characterize themselves as *anti-alchemists,* nor do astronomers call themselves *anti-astrologers.** If one defines psychiatry con-

---

* The term *anti-psychiatry* is not only not good, it is also not new. It was used as early as 1912 by Bernhard Beyer to characterize an article critical of psychiatry.[2]

ventionally, as the medical specialty concerned with the diagnosis and treatment of mental diseases, then one is, indeed, committed to "opposing" psychiatry as a specialty—not of medicine but of mythology. However, since I believe that people are entitled to their mythologies, this opposition must be clearly limited to the use of force or fraud by the mythologizers in the pursuit of their ersatz religion. This is why I have always insisted that I am against involuntary psychiatry, or the psychiatric rape of the patient by the psychiatrist—but I am not against voluntary psychiatry, or psychiatric relations between consenting adults.

On the other hand, if one defines psychiatry operationally, as consisting of whatever psychiatrists do, then it is necessary to identify and articulate one's attitude toward each of the numerous practices in which psychiatrists engage. I have tried to do this in several of my publications, always indicating what I oppose, what I support, and why. As against this analytical approach, the very term *anti-psychiatry* implicitly commits one to opposing everything that psychiatrists do—which is patently absurd. In any case, anti-psychiatrists do not clearly state whether they object only to involuntary psychiatric interventions, or also to those that are voluntary; to all involuntary psychiatric interventions, or only to those practiced by their political adversaries. They do not frankly acknowledge whether they support real tolerance for contractual psychiatric interventions, or only "repressive tolerance" for (against) them—because such practices occur in an "exploitative-capitalist" context of free market and free enterprise.

Actually, as we shall see, the anti-psychiatrists are all self-declared socialists, communists, or at least anticapitalists and collectivists. As the communists seek to raise the poor above the rich, so the anti-psychiatrists seek to raise the "insane" above the "sane"; as the communists justify their aims and methods by claiming that the poor are virtuous, while the rich

49

are wicked, so the anti-psychiatrists justify theirs by claiming that the "insane" are authentic, while the "sane" are inauthentic.

Ronald Laing, who with David Cooper originated the so-called anti-psychiatry movement, began his work with the study of schizophrenic persons. His first book, published in 1960, is titled *The Divided Self* [3]—an almost literal translation of the Bleulerian Greek term *schizophrenia,* and a virtual repetition of the classic psychiatric view of the schizophrenic as a "split personality." Four years later, with Aaron Esterson, Laing published *Sanity, Madness, and the Family.* Subtitled *Families of Schizophrenics,* [4] it is a report on the study of eleven hospitalized schizophrenic patients and their families. Nowhere in this book do the authors identify the legal status of any of the "schizophrenics"—that is, whether they are voluntary or involuntary patients. There is also no mention of what, if any, roles Laing and Esterson played in depriving these persons of their liberty, or, if they were deprived of their liberty by others, what, if any, roles the two authors played in trying to help them to regain it.

Subsequently, Laing has, on some occasions, rejected the idea that schizophrenia is a disease, but he has continued to "treat" it. The fame of Kingsley Hall—Laing's "asylum" for managing madness—rests almost entirely on the claim that it offers a method of helping "schizophrenic patients" superior to those offered by other psychiatric institutions or practitioners.

I have long maintained, and continue to insist, that if there is no disease, there is *nothing* to treat; if there is no patient, there is *no one* to treat. Insofar as others make the same claim—that is, that schizophrenia (and mental illness generally) is not a disease—they are compelled, by the logic of language alone, to conclude also that there is no "treatment" for it. However, inasmuch as many persons whom psychiatrists diagnose as schizophrenic seek help—especially if "help" is not forced on them and if they don't have to pay for it—we are confronted with the social reality of "psychotics," supposedly lacking "insight" into their "illness," clamoring for its "treatment."

Laing accepts such persons as "residents" in his "communities " and legitimizes them as "sufferers" who, because of their very "victimization," are more worthy than others. There is thus built into his system of asylum care a moral-economic premise which is inexplicit but is all the more important for being so. It is, moreover, the same premise that animates large numbers of men and women today throughout the civilized world. Briefly put, it is the premise that it is wicked for people to purchase, for money, medical or psychiatric (or anti-psychiatric) help, but it is virtuous to "purchase" it for suffering. I shall say more about this moral dimension of the therapeutic nexus presently. Here it should suffice to note that in espousing this position, Laing is hardly unconventional. On the contrary, he places himself squarely midstream of the main current of contemporary thought and sentiment about "health care." This current, in both communist and capitalist countries, is now fully Marxist—adopting, for "suffering situations," * the famous formula: "From each according to his abilities, to each according to his needs."

Economically, Laing has thus replaced the coercion of the mental patient by the psychiatrist on behalf of the citizen, with the coercion of the taxpayer by the government on behalf of the mental patient. Formerly, sane citizens could *detain* those whom they considered to be mad; now they must *maintain* those who undertake to "journey" through madness.

I say this because even if a person is, in his current situation, unmolested by his family and employer, by the police and psychiatry—in other words, even if he is not actually harassed or persecuted in any way whatever—Laing still accepts

* The expression is Kenneth Minogue's.[5]

him as a resident at Kingsley Hall and legitimizes him as a bona fide sufferer. I am not contending that such persons may not, in fact, suffer—at least in the sense in which most persons often suffer from the slings and arrows of outrageous fortune. I am contending only that it does not follow logically or morally that such persons are entitled to services extracted by force or fraud from others—whether those "others" be indentured torturers in old-fashioned state hospitals or indentured taxpayers in new-fashioned welfare states. I am trying to make explicit here something which, so far as I know, is never made explicit either by Laing and his followers, or by their critics —namely, that the cost of the care of the "residents" in the Laingian asylums is mainly borne by the British taxpayer; and that the British taxpayer has no more of a direct vote on whether or not he wants his hard-earned money spent that way than did the American taxpayer on paying for the war in Vietnam. Ironically, while Laing's tongue lashes society for driving people mad, his hands are picking the taxpayers' pockets.

Furthermore, anti-psychiatrists resemble psychiatrists and psychoanalysts in their insistent inattention to whether the so-called mental patient assumes his role voluntarily or is assigned to it against his will. Psychoanalysts, psychiatrists, and anti-psychiatrists all theorize about neurosis and psychosis, hysteria and schizophrenia, without acknowledging whether persons so identified seek or avoid psychiatric help; whether they accept or reject being diagnosed; whether they claim to be suffering or others impute suffering to them. Thus all of these seemingly different, and sometimes even antagonistic, approaches to so-called psychiatric problems display this crucial similarity: each regards the "patient" as a "case"—indeed, as a "victim." To the psychiatrist, the "schizophrenic" is a victim of an elusive disease of the brain, like neurosyphilis; to the psychoanalyst he is a victim of a weak ego, a powerful id, or a combination of both; and to the anti-psychiatrist he is a victim of an intrusive family and an insane society. Each of these creeds and cults diminishes and distorts the "patient" as the person he really is; each denies his self-explanatory act of self-definition. Thus, the psychiatrist denies the "schizophrenic's" right to reject confinement, and attributes his desire for freedom to lack of insight into his illness and his need for treatment of it; the psychoanalyst denies his right to resist analytic interpretation, and attributes his noncooperation with the analyst to an "illness" that renders him "inaccessible" to analysis; and the anti-psychiatrist denies his obligation to care for himself and to obey the law, and views his penchant for social rule violation as proof of his superior moral virtue.

The result is a lumping together—in psychoanalysis, psychiatry, and anti-psychiatry—of the most dissimilar kinds of persons. For example, persons able but unwilling to take care of themselves are placed in the same class with those willing but unable to do so; persons who are guilty but claim to be innocent are placed in the same class with those who are innocent but claim to be guilty; and persons charged with and convicted of lawbreaking are placed in the same class with those who are neither charged with nor convicted of any offense. In psychiatry and psychoanalysis, each of these types of persons may be categorized as "schizophrenic"; in anti-psychiatry, such categorization of persons as "schizophrenics" is, on the one hand, criticized as erroneous, and on the other hand, embraced as identifying a specific group of individuals distinctively victimized by others and especially suitable for Laingian methods of mental treatment. In all of these ways, the similarities among psychiatry, psychoanalysis, and anti-psychiatry in their approach to "schizophrenia" seem to me to far outweigh the differences among them.

In short, insofar as anti-psychiatry is a continuation of the tradition of moral treatment in psychiatry, it is nothing new; insofar as it is a political perspective on society and a set of practical policies about human relations, it is an inversion of certain Western values and arrangements. Some of these points have been made before by critics of anti-psychiatry, most cogently by David Martin and Lionel Trilling.

The gist of Martin's argument, with which I am in substantial agreement, is that Laing is a preacher of and for the "soft" underbelly of the New Left. By "soft New Leftism" Martin means, among other things, a "syndrome of attitudes" which confronts us with a "psychological set that positively avoids careful analysis and treats the notion of fact as a treacherous bourgeois invention." [6] Laing's "predominant style," adds Martin, "is not 'honourable argument': instead it is gnomic, testamental, and confessional." [7] Martin calls attention to Laing's recurrent references "to the nature of capitalist society as being a near-universal social context in which freedom is deformed," [8] and notes that this is a rather absurd assertion, not because it is completely false, but because it is less true of contemporary capitalist societies than of any other societies, past or present, about which we know anything. But, as Martin emphasizes, the whole point of Laing's style is to avoid and undercut the development of an exchange of reasoned assertions and denials.[9]

Here, I might add, lies one of the most important similarities between traditional psychiatrists and Laingian anti-psychiatrists: one cannot reason or argue with any of them. Each is like a religious zealot with whom one cannot discuss or debate anything that touches on his creed. Such a person permits only two options: total agreement and total disagreement. In the former case one is allowed to acknowledge the psychiatrist or anti-psychiatrist as the possessor of true insight into the heart and mind of the psychotic and the defender of the psychotic's own best interests. In the latter one is demeaned and degraded by an invidious "diagnosis," that is, by being declared mad—the victim of insanity or inauthenticity.

All of anti-psychiatry is characterized by this fateful similarity to what it opposes. In traditional psychiatry, "we" are sane and "they," who defy the norms and values of our society, are insane. In anti-psychiatry it is the other way around. "There is in Laing's writing," remarks Martin, "not a single word suggesting that any virtue inheres in what is his own inheritance." [10] That is almost putting it too mildly, for Laing is fond of tossing off remarks such as: "the worst barbarities are still perpetrated by 'ourselves,' by our 'allies' and 'friends.' " [11] This total rejection of "us," and the complementary romanticization of "them," is, of course, characteristic of the contemporary "leftist" mentality in the still "free" societies.

The image of Laing that emerges from Martin's analysis of his work is that of an angry prophet, an intolerant religious fanatic, hurling in our faces such accusations and challenges as this: "We are all murderers and prostitutes. . . . " [12] According to Martin, Laing is

> an irrationalist in that he finds rational and argued discussion of religious questions uncongenial, and insists that the essence of religion is ecstasy. . . . There is in Laing's whole style a *substitution* of ecstasy for argument and a disinclination to build up a sequence of ordered points, supported by carefully collected evidence, qualified in respect to this issue or that. His method consists in random accusation and sloganized virulence, which destroys the possibility of discussion. [13]

In short, like the mad-doctors of yore and the psychoanalysts of only yesterday, Laing is a base rhetorician. [14]

Lionel Trilling has also noted that Laing's criticism of the existing social order is similar, in all essential respects, to that of Marxism and Communism, and that the salvation he proposes for it resembles the solutions offered by these collectivistic creeds. Although I do not agree with Trilling's uncritical acceptance of schizophrenia as a disease (he seems to think that it is just like syphilis, only more difficult to diagnose), I regard most of his criticism of anti-psychiatry as valid and important.

Thus, Trilling is right in reemphasizing—indeed, I think his emphasis is not nearly strong enough—the economic nexus into which the anti-psychiatry movement belongs, and into which it must be explicitly reinserted. That nexus is Marxian anticapitalism. In it, Trilling remarks, "money is the principle of the inauthentic in human existence." [15] He cites Oscar Wilde's remark, apropos of this new vision of the genuinely "human being," that "The true perfection of man lies not in what man has but in what man is." [16] It then follows, as Trilling himself suggests, that the moral ideal is no longer that a man should *know himself,* but that he should *be himself.* This sounds nice so long as we do not ask what it means. For what is concealed in this prescription is nothing less than the whole meaning and value of life itself.

Laing's theory of schizophrenia, which serves as the moral justification and economic foundation for whatever work he does as a helper or healer, thus rests on the idea of inauthenticity and its role in this "disorder." It is precisely on this point that Trilling delivers his most damaging blows against Laing's work:

> Schizophrenia, in his [Laing's] view, is the consequence of an external circumstance, an influence exerted upon the sense of selfhood, of a person who is more disposed than others to yield to it; the schizophrenic person characteristically has what Laing calls an "ontological insecurity," a debility of his sentiment of being. . . . It is the family which is directly responsible for the ontological break, the "divided self" of schizophrenia; Laing is categorical in saying

that every case of schizophrenia is to be understood as "a special strategy that the patient invents in order to live an unlivable situation," which is always a family situation, specifically the demand of parents that one be what one is not. We may put it that Laing construes schizophrenia as the patient's response to the parental imposition of inauthenticity.[17]

Trilling here puts his sensitive finger on the nonsensical and mischievous aspects of the cult of authenticity. This cult is, in some ways, the mirror image of the cult of modern institutional psychiatry. As in psychiatry the core concept, the sacred symbol, is "schizophrenia," so in anti-psychiatry it is "authenticity." In the former view, what the schizophrenic has less of than other people is the ability to "test reality"; in the latter view, what the schizophrenic has more of than other people is "authenticity."

Given the problems that the "schizophrenic" presents to himself and others, and given Laing's perspective of attributing all human problems to society, it was inevitable, according to Trilling, that the cause of schizophrenia "be sought in social factors. . . . [But it] . . . was not inevitable . . . that this line of thought should issue in the verdict that insanity is a state of human existence which is to be esteemed for its commanding authenticity." [18]

This is, indeed, a most unfortunate claim. By making it, Laing and Cooper, and those who support their idealization of insanity, have, in my opinion, done a great disservice to the cause of enlarging the sphere of human decency for all people—regardless of whether they are psychotics or psychiatrists, both or neither. The proposition that the madman is sane and that society is insane is the sort of thing that Trilling calls *cant*. In my view, it is not just cant, but rather counter-cant: it is the echo of the psychiatric cant which categorizes disagreement as disease—which Trilling seems to think is a scientific proposition. But Trilling is right in emphasizing that cant cannot be countered with logic. Many a "schizophrenic" has discovered this, as has many a would-be critic of "scientific" psychiatry. Trilling observes:

> To deal with this phenomenon of our intellectual culture in the way of analytical argument would, I think, be supererogatory. The position may be characterized as being in an intellectual mode to which analytical argument is not appropriate. This is the intellectual mode that once went under the name of cant. The disappearance of the word from the modern vocabulary is worth remarking.[19]

The disappearance of this word, and also of *rhetoric,* is, of course, intimately related to the acceptance and growth of psychiatry as a "science," a subject on which I have remarked at length elsewhere.[20]

Trilling cites passages from Cooper and Laing to illustrate what he means by anti-psychiatric cant. For a fully balanced view of schizophrenia—from Kraepelin and Bleuler to the present—we must be as clear and critical of the cant of anti-psychiatry as we are of that of psychiatry; and for a fully humane—by which term I mean a candid, contractual, noncoercive—policy toward schizophrenia, we must reject the blandishments of anti-psychiatry as firmly as we do the punishments of psychiatry.

We can all recognize psychiatric cant: it is the material that comes packaged between the covers of textbooks of psychiatry (and psychoanalysis). Anti-psychiatric cant is the same thing, turned upside down or inside out. Trilling cites this example of it from Cooper's Introduction to Foucault's *Madness and Civilization:*

> Madness . . . is a way of seizing *in extremis* the racinating groundwork of the truth that underlies our more specific realization of what we are about. The truth of madness is what madness is, what madness is is a form of vision that destroys itself by its own choice of oblivion in the face of existing forms of social tactics and strategy. Madness, for instance, is a matter of voicing the realization that I am (or you are) Christ.[21]

Actually, it is easy to cite even more blatant passages of cant from Cooper's writings, as well as from Laing's. For example, in *The Death of the Family* Cooper declares that "all lethal diseases are suicide in the sense of refusal to love." [22] Cooper here confuses himself not only with Jesus Christ but also with Georg Groddeck, who came to believe that all human diseases were due to mental conflicts.

"The bourgeois state," Cooper explains, "is a tranquilizer pill with lethal side effects." [23] His prescription for "liberation" from it is equally illuminating:

> The fulfillment of liberation comes only with effective macropolitical action. So the Centers of Revolutionary Consciousness have also to become Red Bases. Macropolitical action here must be essentially negative, and takes the form of rendering bourgeois power structures impotent by any and every means. . . . Molotov cocktails certainly have their place in a significantly organized, student-worker rebellion. . . . [24]

Cooper's comments about "Red Bases" and "Molotov cocktails" are not just asides, tossed off to impress the intellectual lumpen proletariat; they constitute a consistent theme, both in *The Dialectics of Liberation* and *The Death of the Family*. In the former book he eulogizes the North Vietnamese guerrillas, refers to Cuba as "already liberated," and to the impending communist conquest in Vietnam as putting that country "inexorably on the way to liberation." [25] In the latter, his enmity toward capitalist leaders is as unqualified as is his endorsement of communist leaders:

> False leaders are simply shadowy presences, with artificial, "big man" images regurgitated by non-human, institutionalized social processes—for example the Hitlers, Churchills, Kennedys, etc. The true leadership principle is embodied in men like Fidel Castro and Mao Tse-tung, who lead by almost refusing to be leaders. . . .[26]

Laing's political cant has the same ring: "we" are wicked, and "they" are virtuous. In his interview with Richard Evans he offers this revealing remark about some recent atrocities:

> In the sixties, the military struggle in Indochina was far more extensive than was being let on. Cambodia was being bombed. God knows what else is going on there now. Look at the German bystander apathy about the concentration camps. Look at the British apathy when their bomber command destroyed a city like Dresden just to show the Americans and Russians what the British Air Force could do.[27]

Neither Cooper nor Laing leave us in any doubt concerning what they and their anti-psychiatry are all about: they seek, by methods even more fanatical and ferocious than those they wish to replace, to impose their particular values on the world. Cooper's following proposal is typical:

> For the less sophisticated middle-class and working-class men-women relationships (the upper classes being fully and

finally dedicated to nonsexuality), one needs a more totally operating revolutionizing activity in the whole society. This is where acutely posed strikes, bombs, and machine guns will have to come in, with a guiding compassion but also a certain reality that is wholly objective, seen and felt, by the agents of bourgeois society, towards whom we can only be compassionate at a second remove.[28]

Kraepelin and Bleuler on the psychiatric "right"; Laing and Cooper on the psychiatric "left." They match each other by their apparent antagonisms which conceal their actual agreements: each is convinced of the absolute righteousness of his respective position and of his right, indeed duty, to impose his will on those who resist him—by whatever force may be necessary. Kraepelin conceals imprisonment as hospitalization and calls it psychiatry; Cooper conceals killing the "agents of bourgeois society" and waging revolution with bombs and machine guns as liberation guided by compassion and calls it anti-psychiatry. Not in their wildest moments, however, did the ambitions of the traditional psychiatrists approximate those of the modern anti-psychiatrists. We might call this, or at least think of it, as the Romanoff-Lenin effect, which I would define as follows: He who liberates you despotically from another despot will surpass in his cruelty the worst cruelties of his erstwhile antagonist.

I think we owe it to Cooper to take him seriously, and to draw from his writings the conclusions clearly implicit in them. Cooper himself cannot be faulted; he has made them explicit enough:

All deaths in the first world are murder disguised as suicide disguised as the course of Nature. . . . Revolution, I believe, will only be a total enough social reality when white men can assume all the colors of blackness and then have babies too. In Cuba, the Guevarist doctrine of the New Man gets very close to the extended sense of revolution that I have pursued in these pages. The New Man is the pragmatic revolutionary who effectively annihilates the power structures of the feudal, bourgeois state and takes whatever power he needs to maintain an autonomous community. . . .[29]

In short, Cooper's prescription for the conquest of insanity, alienation, poverty, and every other human misery is the old apocalyptic-millenarian dream of the collectivist "brotherhood" of men and women all over the world. It is an old dream that has, since the French Revolution, turned into a nightmare, and worse, for countless people all over the world.

As I noted, both Martin and Trilling emphasize that Laing does not reason or argue; he blames and preaches. Accordingly, there is not the slightest effort in his works, or in those of the other anti-psychiatrists, at consistency. There is no schizophrenia, but they treat it. The sane are madder than the insane, but they operate asylums for the latter, not the former. The capitalist West is more oppressive than the communist East, but all these anti-psychiatrists live in, and off, the former, and stay carefully clear of the latter.

One of the most interesting and informative documents in this connection is the *Philadelphia Association Report, 1965–1969*. This is the organization founded by or under the guidance of Ronald Laing in 1965, for the purpose of providing asylum for—what should we call them?—schizophrenics, homeless persons, "victims." Let us see how the report handles this matter of naming the "clients" and their "caretakers."

Faithfully following the style of contemporary Western collectivism, the report has no identified or identifiable authors, and the asylums it operates have no identified staff. Indeed, individualism, self-identification as a form of self-aggrandizement, is denounced at the outset, in the dedication, which reads as follows:

> This report arises from the communal experience of many people who agreed to be together without predefined professional or social roles. To all of them, too numerous to name, this report is dedicated.[30]

Just what, then, is the Philadelphia Association? It is "A Registered National Charity in the United Kingdom," and an organization which has secured for itself exemption "from United States income tax under Section 501(C)(3) of the Internal Revenue Code." [31] The purposes of the Association are set forth in its "Articles of Association" as follows:

> To relieve mental illness of all descriptions, in particular schizophrenia.
>
> To undertake, or further, research into the causes of mental illness, the means of its detection and prevention, and its treatment.
>
> To provide, or further the provision of, residential accommodations for persons suffering or who have suffered from mental illness.
>
> To provide financial assistance for poor patients.
>
> To promote and organize training in the treatment of schizophrenia and other forms of mental illness.[32]

This could just as well have been written by Karl Menninger as by Ronald Laing. It sounds like Laing's attempt to set up his version of the Menninger Clinic; that is, his factory (called "residential accommodations" instead of "hospital beds") for manufacturing mental patients (called "schizophrenics" in both cases), and for training future factory workers and managers (called "training" persons in "the treatment of schizophrenia and other forms of mental illness" in both cases).

The first business of the Philadelphia Association was to lease a building called Kingsley Hall for the purpose of turning it into a "residential accommodation" or "asylum." Kingsley Hall, which opened its doors in June 1965, has, we are told,

> no staff, patients, or institutional procedures. . . . Behaviour is feasible there which is intolerable in most other places. People get up or stay in bed as they wish, eat what they want when they want, stay alone or be with others, and generally make their own rules.[33]

There are, at least according to this report, no obligations or duties of any kind placed upon the "residents." Above all, they need not pay for anything they receive. Or, if they have to pay for it, it is not mentioned. What is mentioned, indeed emphasized, is that:

> Many residents are poor, with only social security benefits. No one has been turned away for financial reasons, despite our limited resources. However, activities are restricted when funds are low.[34]

In short, Kingsley Hall differs from the Menninger Clinic (or any other private mental hospital) in much the same way that a flophouse differs from a first-class hotel. In each case, room and board are provided by one group of persons for another, regardless of what each group calls itself or the other.

Thus, toward money, too, Laing displays the same pious posture as do institutional psychiatrists. The traditional asylum psychiatrist imposed a nonreciprocal economic relationship on the madman, ostensibly treating him as a "solicitous" father treats his "needy" child, while actually receiving payment for his services from others. The same economic arrangement characterizes the triangular relations of guides, voyagers, and dispensers of funds in the Laingian asylums. Both settings reek of the odor of therapeutic sanctimoniousness which the "conceit of philanthropy" * inevitably exudes.

Laing imposes no explicit financial obligation on the "patients" at Kingsley Hall. Regardless of how much money the patient may have, or of how much he may spend on liquor, tobacco, or gambling, he does not have to spend any of it on paying for "mental health care." How, then, does he gauge whether the patient is deserving of care? By measuring his "need" in terms of his suffering and his willingness to submit to his helpers. This paternalistic posture has long been held to be the cornerstone of the ideal model of medical ethics. It is the role which Laing and his disciples blindly embrace, thus displaying the same contempt for their charges as the keepers of madmen at the Burghölzli, Maudsley, or Salpêtrière have always displayed.

It is clear, then, that what Laing and Cooper oppose is not so much any particular psychiatric intervention as the principle of making and keeping promises; not so much coercion as contract. In short, what they oppose is not "therapeutic" caprice, but predictable rules binding equally—morally as well as legally—on all contracting parties.

Sooner or later, it seems to me, we must all choose between the two dominant principles for regulating human relations—that is, between contracts and commands.[36] Confronted with this choice, Laing and Cooper come down squarely in support of commands and in opposition to contracts. In this crucially important respect, too, they stand shoulder to shoulder with the traditional psychiatric authorities whom they seek to overthrow and replace. The similarities between the Laingian asylum and the lunatic asylum go even further, as I shall presently show.

* The phrase is William F. May's.[35]

There are troubling inconsistencies not only between Laing's assertion that schizophrenia is not a disease and his claim that he possesses a superior method of treating it, but also between the Philadelphia Association's claim that Kingsley Hall has no professional staff or hierarchy and Laing's self-identification, in the journal *The Human Context,* as "Director, Kingsley Hall (Clinic)." [37] In short, instead of demystifying the metaphors of medicine, Laing alternately denounces them in a philosophically sweeping and politically selective way, and uses them for all they are worth by deploying them as his own rhetorical devices.

Reflections such as these have made me conclude that in the psychiatric war with words, the metaphors of medicine do the work of hand grenades; the present positions of psychiatrists and anti-psychiatrists are like those of soldiers in trenches facing each other, lobbing the same grenades back and forth, hoping they will go off in their enemies' faces rather than in their own. I am opposed to this sort of use of the medical vocabulary, regardless of the identity of the user.

Clearly, the anti-psychiatrists have accepted the central role of schizophrenia in psychiatry. What they have done, essentially, is to invert its position and significance, casting blame on the family and society instead of on the patient and his disease. They have thus argued that society, not the schizophrenic, is insane; indeed, that the schizophrenic is, at least some times, supersane, in the sense that, because he is a "victim," he is ipso facto more virtuous than his victimizers.

My argument against psychiatry proceeds from quite different premises and points to quite different conclusions. My primary charge against psychiatry has been aimed at the things psychiatrists actually do, and my secondary charge at their claims concerning what psychotics supposedly suffer from. Briefly put, I have maintained that the intervention institutional psychiatrists call "mental hospitalization" is, in fact, a form of imprisonment; that the imposition of such loss of liberty on innocent persons is immoral (and, in the United States, unconstitutional); and that the phenomenon psychiatrists call "schizophrenia" is not a demonstrable medical disease but the name of certain kinds of social deviance (or of behavior unacceptable to the speaker).

While there is no need to encumber this presentation with a detailed retelling of the story of Mary Barnes, some remarks on it are essential for a rounded view of the doctrines and deceptions of anti-psychiatry.

Mary Barnes is to anti-psychiatry what the Wolfman is to psychoanalysis: each is the movement's most famous case, its most eloquent testimonial witness to the miraculous powers of its leader. The book, *Mary Barnes: Two Accounts of a Journey Through Madness,*[38] consists of two parts, one written by Mary Barnes, the "tourist," the other by Joseph Berke, her "guide." It provides "penetrating glimpses" not so much into the "inner world of the schizophrenic," as the publisher's blurb promises, as into the inner sanctum of Kingsley Hall, the holy mosque of anti-psychiatry.

The advertisement for the book promises one thing and implies another, both important. It promises new revelations about Laing's special method for treating schizophrenia. It implies that there are certain similarities between this account and other testimonials of miraculous recoveries from madness, with the difference that this time, at last, psychiatry—or rather anti-psychiatry—has schizophrenia really licked.

The top line of the publisher's blurb, quoting from a review in *Publishers Weekly,* reads: "One of the most penetrating glimpses into innovative psychotherapy techniques." [39] Then follows the publisher's own text, presumably approved by the authors and Laing:

> Two views of the inner world of a schizophrenic, told by the patient and the psychiatrist who helped her back to health when they lived and worked together in R. D. Laing's therapeutic community, Kingsley Hall.[40]

Nearly every word in this blurb belies Laing's claims and the claims of those who work at Kingsley Hall:

1. Laing says that there is no schizophrenia and that there are no schizophrenics; yet here we are offered not one view but two of the "inner world of a schizophrenic."

2. The communards at Kingsley Hall claim that there are no patients and psychiatrists there; yet here we are told that there are.

3. The operators of this asylum claim that it is not owned or controlled by any one person, but is a communal enterprise; yet here it is explicitly identified as "R. D. Laing's."

4. Laing and his followers claim that the schizophrenic is not sick; yet here we are offered the account of a schizophrenic restored to "health" in a "therapeutic community."

It would be difficult, even if one tried, to pack more contradictions about Laing's claims and the anti-psychiatry movement's confusions into a few sentences.

Laing's role in Mary Barnes' sojourn at Kingsley Hall, where she was cared for during her psychosis, is indicated at several points in the account, beginning in the Acknowledgments, where Berke writes:

> I would like to acknowledge my indebtedness to Ronald Laing for many of the concepts which I discuss and illustrate throughout my account. I refer, most particularly, to the

awareness that psychosis may be a state of reality, cyclic in nature, by which the self renews itself; and to the awareness that a person may function at several levels of regression at the same time.[41]

These ideas belong of course, to Jung and Federn, and to Freud, rather than to Laing. As for Mary Barnes, she offers this revealing observation:

Unable to cope in ways that "grown-up" people used, I seemed at sea. Ronnie once said at dinner to the other people: "Mary has no ego boundaries." Just in going my own ways, being as I was seemed at times to make other people angry. Then I was surprised: "Why Joe, I'm just getting on with myself." [42]

It is interesting that Laing prefers to speak about Mary Barnes in psychoanalytic jargon, rather than in ordinary language. Her remarks suggest that the "attendants" at Kingsley Hall are not much more tolerant of psychotic coercions than are attendants in ordinary mental hospitals. Moreover, Mary Barnes' passion to control and be controlled is as plain as Laing's and Berke's passion to plagiarize psychoanalytic concepts. She writes: "Not to be possessed and controlled can be very frightening. The hospital with its drugs and physical treatments and compulsory admission is controlling and possessing." In a footnote she adds: "I use the word hospital in the usual accepted way. To me the word denotes a place of healing, of therapy. Kingsley Hall is, in this sense, a real, true hospital." [43]

Mary Barnes, the true believer in the metaphorization of personal problems as medical maladies, here asserts herself. She is sick. Kingsley Hall is a hospital. Berke and Laing are doctors. She has made them act out the roles she wished to impose on them. Laing's theorizing is, from this perspective, an effort to deny his actual relationship with persons such as Mary Barnes:

a relationship based not on informed consent and economic contract, but on mutual coercion and celebration.

Laing begins and ends *The Politics of Experience* in a way that seems to me revealing of his moral style and vision. The style is arrogant and mystical; the vision, apocalyptic and threatening. His opening sentences are:

> Few books today are forgivable. Black on the canvas, silence on the screen, an empty white sheet of paper, are perhaps feasible. There is little conjunction of truth and social "reality." [44]

Does this sort of writing betoken the acceptance of psychosis and of the psychotic? Why this arbitrary and absurd condemnation of other people's writings? For it is quite clear that Laing regards his own books as "forgivable" and "feasible," and more. He also likes books written about him, although the trees cut down to make them possible make his ecological heart bleed. "We shall cut down God knows how many trees to have one edition of this book," he tells Evans. "The mind boggles at what we're doing." [45]

One of the characteristics of Laing's personal and literary style is his penchant for saying and writing things without asserting anything. It is what Trilling calls cant, but it is a particular kind of cant—one that fairly reeks of the odor of conceit and self-importance. Here is a sample: "I haven't met anyone with a mind quite like mine. It's somewhat original." [46]

Of course, Laing does make some assertions, and many of them are astonishing indeed. For example:

> The military are very interested in telepathy, hypnosis, etc. . . . There's a throb, or beat, a pulse between us that the

grabby, manipulating fingers of the military-medical-scientific-industrial complex is just beginning to get hold of. The swamis are being wired up. Magic voodoo? Primitive. Hitler and his astrologists. In fact, we now know that World War II was largely programmed, astrologically, by Hitler's astrological advisers. Churchill employed a state astrologer to advise him on what Hitler's astrologers were doing.[47]

Perhaps because we all "know" these things, Laing supplies no references identifying the sources of these "facts." However, he does at least tell us something important about himself—namely, that "The contract I have made with my mind is that it is free to do anything it cares to do." [48]

Laing may be a genius at making contracts with his own mind, but there is no evidence of his even trying to make and keep real promises to real people, or of his trying to negotiate and consummate real contracts with real contracting parties.[49] Such predictability and reliability is simply not a part of his self-image or personal style. This explains why Laing systematically avoids specifying what he himself considers to be the duties of "therapists" or "guides" vis-à-vis "patients" or "tourists," and vice versa.

Moreover, Laing also "lets us know" that he is not satisfied with conveying his image of "reality," but that, if he had his way, only he (and perhaps a few others) could put ink marks on "white sheets of paper"; that, in short, he wants not to communicate but to convert. In the concluding sentence of *The Politics of Experience* he declares: "If I could turn you on, if I could drive you out of your wretched mind, if I could tell you I would let you know." [50]

There is thus a consistent symmetry between the old psychiatry and the new anti-psychiatry. In psychiatry the dominant imagery was that of man "losing his mind." Curing him meant, therefore, helping him to "find the mind he lost"; if he refused to find it by following the psychiatrist's guidance, then it meant "driving" him back into it. In anti-psychiatry the dominant imagery is that of man having a "false" or "wrong mind." Curing him means, therefore, helping him to "lose" his false consciousness or inauthentic self; if he refuses to lose it or to give it up by following the anti-psychiatrist's guidance, then it means "driving" him out of his "wretched mind."

To be sure, occasionally Laing says almost exactly what I say about schizophrenia—namely, that there is no such thing, that schizophrenia is a name and a metaphor.[51] But then, almost as if it were enough to pay lip service to this idea, he acclaims again and again the schizophrenic's superiority over ordinary people. Here is a typical passage:

> The [future men] will see that what we call "schizophrenia" was one of the forms in which, often through quite ordinary people, the light began to break through the cracks in our all-too-closed minds.[52]

Laing often repeats this idea. We must assume, therefore, that he means it, that it is an integral part of his vision of psychiatry and of the so-called problem of schizophrenia. But, of course, schizophrenia cannot be *both* a metaphorical illness and a psychopathological state defined by those who use the term as a literalized metaphor! Yet Laing consistently treats schizophrenia as both, without ever bothering to identify, much less to define, what it is that he refers to when, for example, he asserts that "madness need not be all breakdown. It may also be break-through." [53] That sounds nice. Much nicer than Bleuler. But it is not a whit more informative, as Laing has absolutely nothing to say about which madnesses are breakdowns and why, which are breakthroughs and why, and how we distinguish one from the other when we see them. In short, Laing continues in the tradition of Bleuler and Freud insofar as he has his own categories of approved and disapproved conduct—he even calls them "sanity" and "madness"!—but does not tell us, clearly and unequivocally, what they are or how we can identify them.

The impression that, despite its verbal concealments, Laing's actual position on schizophrenia is quite close not only to Bleuler's but also to Freud's is also strongly supported by Laing's "Wolfwoman"—Mary Barnes. Consider the parallels. As Freud had a famous patient psychoanalyzed on the couch, so Laing has one guided through madness at Kingsley Hall. As the Wolfman had a "neurosis," which is the sacred symbol of psychoanalysis, so Mary Barnes had a "psychosis," which is the sacred symbol of psychiatry and anti-psychiatry. And, finally, as Freud's famous patient and the legends about him and other patients authenticated Freud as an exceptional healer of neurotics, so Laing's famous patient and the legends about her and other patients authenticate Laing as an exceptional healer of psychotics.

The general structural similarities between asylum psychiatry and anti-psychiatry are equally arresting. The lunatic asylums were run by one set of people for the benefit of another; so are the Laingian asylums. The people who ran the lunatic asylum insisted that their establishment was a hospital, that they were doctors, and that their clients were patients; the inmates maintained that they were confined in prison, that their keepers were jailers, and that they were prisoners. The people who run the Laingian asylum insist that their establishment is a hostel, that they are guides, and that their clients are tourists lost on their journey through madness; the inmates maintain that they are treated in a hospital, that their superiors are doctors, and that they are patients.

The struggle over definitions is much the same in the lunatic and the Laingian asylums; there is a similar disjunction between keeper and kept in each, the former insisting on his medical or antimedical definitions of himself and his client, the latter on his complementarily antagonistic antimedical and medical definitions of himself and his keepers. As against these similarities, the main differences between them is that in the lunatic asylum the guiding metaphors were medical, whereas in the Laingian they are Alpinistic, and that in the former, relations of domination-submission, coercion-countercoercion were concealed by the imagery of lost minds being restored to "sanity," while in the latter they are concealed by lost tourists being restored to "true sanity." Plus ça change, plus c'est la même chose.*

Mary Barnes' "recovery" thus depended, it seems to me, not on her being "guided through a journey through madness," but rather on her ability to manipulate her therapists—and their willingness to be manipulated by her; and on her eagerness to play the role of special patient, saved at Kingsley Hall—and her therapists' desire to cast, and commercialize, her in that role. In all these ways Mary Barnes was reinflated, and inflated herself, with self-esteem. A crucial aspect of her relationship to Laing, Berke,

---

* Schizophrenia *is* no more a journey through madness than it *is* a disease of the brain. Both of these statements assert literalized metaphors. Of course, schizophrenia may be said to be *like* a journey or *like* a disease; but it is also *like* many other conditions or situations, such as being childish, aimless, useless, and homeless, or being angry, obstreperous, conceited, and selfish.

The point is that just as in psychiatry the literalized metaphor of schizophrenia as illness leads to and justifies its management by means of doctors, hospitals, and drugs, so in anti-psychiatry the literalized metaphor of schizophrenia as a journey leads to and justifies its management by means of guides, hostels, and first aid.

What, then, is schizophrenia? For a long time, it has served as the symbol of the sacred mission of psychiatry; now it serves also as the symbol of the sacred mission of anti-psychiatry. Actually, insofar as the term "schizophrenia" designates some "problem" that an ostensible "patient" has, it refers usually to the fact that the "patient's" life is disordered—that it is, or the "patient" thinks it is, aimless and useless. If so, it can no more be "cured" by journeys than by drugs. Chaos, suffering, and turmoil can be remedied only by the subject putting his or her life in order. Whatever helps a person to achieve that goal will be "therapeutic."

and Kingsley Hall thus lay in her transformation from "paranoid schizophrenic," which would have been the demotion diagnosed on her by traditional psychiatry, into "gifted painter," which was the promotion pushed on her by anti-psychiatry. She writes, referring to an artist enlisted as a "guide" in her "journey": "Harry really made me realize that I had been given the gift of God. This moved me, inside. Later, thinking of Harry and Table Mountain, I painted 'Mist, Mountain, and Sea.' " [54]

This is very touching. But it is hardly a conceptual or moral breakthrough in treating children, psychotics, or others who need encouragement and are easy prey for flattery by superior persons on whom they are dependent. It is, rather, another cheap trick—not unlike, as David Martin noted, scoring debating points about making sense out of schizophrenia by making cracks about Vietnam. [55]

And yet, the celebration of Mary Barnes as a "resurrected" person and her discovery as a "gifted" painter are our final crucial clues to the ideology and interventions of anti-psychiatry. When Mary Barnes entered Kingsley Hall she was an undistinguished, unknown, unhappy nurse. When she left, five years later, she was a woman miraculously cured of madness, a gifted painter, a celebrity well on her way toward fame as a goddess in the Church of Anti-Psychiatry. It does not surprise me that she felt better.

As the characteristic operations of institutional psychiatry diminish the mental patient's self-esteem by means of repetitive "degradation ceremonies," so the characteristic operations of anti-psychiatry increase his or her self-esteem by means of repetitive "promotion ceremonies." It surely implies no endorsement of the former to be skeptical about the latter. What are these "promotion ceremonies" about? Do they symbolize the acquisition of knowledge and skills, as do commencement exercises? Or are they ceremonial occasions of a political character, such as coronations? The distinction is important, in ways we cannot consider here. Suffice it to say that there is legitimate reason to doubt that Mary Barnes really learned to paint at Kingsley Hall. In other words, there is legitimate reason to believe that she was not discovered to be a "gifted painter" but merely was declared to be one.

On the front cover of the dust jacket of her book there is a color reproduction of one of Mary Barnes' paintings. Inside the jacket it is identified as: "Spring the Resurrection. A finger painting on a slice of elm, done in the Spring of 1969." [56] I am not an art critic. And even if I were, my judgment about Mary Barnes' talent as a painter might be mistaken or contradicted by others. But I submit that "Spring the Resurrection" is not art; it is "finger painting" defined as art.

Let us view Mary Barnes' "Spring the Resurrection"—the name is again marvelously revealing—as a ceremonial symbol. As the name *schizophrenia* sacralizes—or satanizes—the subject as a madman or madwoman, so the celebration of Mary Barnes' painting sacralizes her as a "gifted painter" or genius. Laing and Cooper should thus be regarded as priests blessing a sacramental object, transforming something ordinary and profane into something extraordinary and holy. And Mary Barnes should be viewed as having been restored to "health" by passage through a classic ritual of purification, confirming her as "saved," her therapists as her "saviors," and Kingsley Hall as the St. Peter's of Anti-Psychiatry.

The anti-psychiatrists' lack of imagination in inverting not only the logic and the vocabulary, but even the trappings, of psychiatry, and appropriating them all as their own "original" theoretical principles and therapeutic methods provokes, in me at least, only contempt and pity. The Freudians discover the smearing of feces in art; [57] the Laingians discover art in the smearing of paint. Or, what comes to the same thing, the psychiatrists seek for the signs of madness, and find them, in the paintings of a genius, such as Vincent van Gogh, whereas the anti-psychiatrists seek for the signs of genius, and find them, in the paintings of madwomen, such as Mary Barnes.

Lock and key fit. The psychiatrist curses and calls it diagnosis, and the patient, especially if he believes it, duly deteriorates. The anti-psychiatrist blesses and calls it discovering genius, and the patient, especially if he believes it, reverently recovers. But how many geniuses can one produce by this method? How many can the market absorb? Is every finger-painting five-year-old really the proto-Picasso his mother thinks he is? Is every Mary Barnes really the Mary Cassatt her Pygmalions claim her to be? Is every young man and woman who is bored and boring, unadmired and unadmirable—or just ordinary—the victim of "plunder"? Has each of them really been robbed of his or her authenticity and sanity, like slaves of their labor and colonized people of their riches? The anti-psychiatrists answer each of these questions with a resounding "yes." But the correct answer, I submit, is "no."

One of the most striking things about Mary Barnes' account of her "journey" is the frank display of her fear of, and escape from, freedom. These felicitous terms are Erich Fromm's,[58] who introduced them to explain the popularity of totalitarian regimes in Europe after the havoc wreaked by World War I. After the havoc that life and their "loved ones" often wreak on individuals, they, too, often develop a desire to escape from freedom. They seek asylum, which is what Kingsley Hall is supposed to be. These parallels between totalitarian regimes and psychiatric asylums, between the fear and rejection of freedom by masses of men and masses of madmen are important—and obvious. Why, then, do I emphasize them? Because although it is obvious that many adults lack freedom not so much because someone has stolen it from them as because they have thrown it away; and although it is equally obvious that persons who act this way may easily get themselves defined as psychotic (especially if that is what they want)—there is, nevertheless, no room in Laing's view of schizophrenia for any of these facts. The schizophrenic, he claims, is always deprived of freedom by others—the family, psychiatry, society. Implicitly, Laing denied that the schizophrenic ever fears freedom because it is too dangerous and demanding, or that he ever deliberately seeks escape from it in the bosom of others—the family, psychiatry, society.

Psychiatry and anti-psychiatry here again fit like lock and key. Psychiatrists deny that involuntary patients ever really want freedom; anti-psychiatrists deny that voluntary tourists ever really want unfreedom. Psychiatrists insist on seeing all schizophrenics, regardless of what they say or do, as sick and needing treatment for madness; anti-psychiatrists insist on seeing all schizophrenics, regardless of what they say or do, as tourists needing a journey through madness.

The anti-psychiatric view here also mirrors faithfully the envious fulminations of modern Marxists and Communists who attribute the poverty of "underdeveloped" peoples to their being robbed, mainly by Americans, of their wealth. The Chileans would all be rich if American companies did not plunder their copper mines. In this anticapitalist perspective, riches flow from natural resources without human intervention. Such intervention only confiscates and corrupts. The Chilean sitting on top of a mountain of unmined copper is "rich." The child left alone with his uncorrupted self is "sane." Each becomes a "victim" through plunder. Cooper articulates this imagery with unashamed naiveté:

Country A (say, the United States of America) buys tomatoes from country B (say, one impoverished South American state), and it sells them back, in tins, to country B at 300 percent profit. This is known as "aid," and aid comes very close to help and treatment. . . .[59]

His ideas on commerce, schizophrenia, and the whole human condition itself, are rooted in the same pattern:

> If one states the schizophrenia problem this way, namely in terms of the existence of a person being sucked out of him by others, or expressed from him by himself (in loving acknowledgment of the others' rapacious ingestion) so that finally nothing of himself is left to himself since he is altogether for the other, then we must conclude that, although being put in hospital represents a special fate, schizophrenia is nothing less than the predicament of each one of us.[60]

Here, at last, is the fully developed image of schizophrenia as the plundered mind. Cooper, of course, overdoes it, as he overdoes everything. Plundering and being plundered are, at least, real, understandable events. People do deprive others of their possessions. But how can everyone be the victim of plunder, which is Cooper's penultimate view of the world. Who, then, are the plunderers? The question is, of course, rhetorical. In the imagery that Laing and Cooper are promoting, we are both victims and victimizers. Who, which, and when is not for us to ask. They will let us know when they are ready.

It should be clear by now that just as the psychiatric paradigm of paresis was not original with Kraepelin and Bleuler and their followers, so the modern anti-psychiatric paradigm is not original with Laing and Cooper and their followers. The psychiatrists have borrowed the disease model from medicine and, on the strength of it, declared psychiatry to be a branch of medicine

—a specialty based on the combination of a medical metaphor and the police power of the state. Similarly, the anti-psychiatrists have borrowed the model of exploitation—of colonialism, foreign invasion, and plunder—from the Old Left and, on the strength of it, declared anti-psychiatry to be a branch of the New Left—a movement based on the combination of a martial metaphor and the persuasive power of apocalyptic promises and prophesies.

Actually, the proposition that the madman is sane but the society that so labels him is insane is merely an extension of Proudhon's famous proposition that "Property is theft." Both make use of the vocabulary of an institution to attack that institution, private property in the one instance, psychiatry in the other. In the former case, according to Searle, "the moral rule or prescription that 'one ought not to steal' can be taken as saying that to recognize something as someone else's property necessarily involves recognizing his right to dispose of it. This is a constitutive rule of the institution of private property." [61] Searle then refers to Proudhon's rule inversion about theft, and comments:

> If one tries to take this as an internal remark it makes no sense. It was intended as an external remark attacking and rejecting the institution of private property. It gets its air of paradox and force by using terms which are internal to the institution in order to attack the institution. Standing on the deck of some institutions one can tinker with constitutive rules and even throw some other institutions overboard. But could one throw all institutions overboard? . . . One could not and still engage in those forms of behavior we consider characteristically human. Suppose Proudhon had added (and tried to live by): "Truth is a lie, marriage is infidelity, language is uncommunicative, law is crime," and so on with every possible institution.[62]

Interestingly, this is exactly what Laing and Cooper have done, and why, in part, they have appealed so strongly to the disaffected youth of our age who, having nothing to live for, are envious of all those who do, and want to destroy the institutions that give meaning to the lives of "normal" people. For my part, I feel just as strongly opposed to individuals demeaning other individuals as insane as a means of gaining meaning for their lives (which is the existential cannibalism characteristic of psychiatry) as I do to individuals demeaning groups or societies as insane (which is the existential cannibalism characteristic of anti-psychiatry).[63]

This, in short, is why I believe that psychiatry and anti-psychiatry are two wrongs, and that two wrongs do not make a right but only a third, still graver, wrong. Psychiatry is a wrong, intellectually—because it interprets disagreement as disease; and morally—because it justifies confinement as cure. Anti-psychiatry is a wrong, intellectually—because it interprets anomie as authenticity; and morally—because by selectively condemning the behavior of our own parents, physicians, and politicians, it justifies the behavior of those, within and outside of our society, who would deprive us of liberty, dignity, and property because they despise us for their own personal or political reasons.

Moreover, psychiatry and anti-psychiatry resemble one another not only as opposites usually do, but also in their shared obsession with "schizophrenia" and its management. This similarity is displayed most strikingly in the dominant images invoked in psychiatry and anti-psychiatry to explain this paradigmatic form of "madness." In psychiatry the dominant image is that the schizophrenic had a "sound mind" but "lost" it. How? By destruction. Like a foreign invader burning down an occupied city and leaving it in ashes, his brain is destroyed by the invading spirochetes of syphilis.

In anti-psychiatry the dominant image is that the schizophrenic had a "sound mind," or could have had one, but was deprived of it or was prevented from developing it. How? By plunder. Like a foreign invader plundering a city and leaving it empty and barren, his personality is "emptied out" by the invading "love" of the family, (capitalist) society, the "oppressors."

In other words, in the psychiatric view of schizophrenia, sanity is synonymous with a biologically healthy brain, which is a nearly universal human possession, and is achieved without personal effort; insanity results from damage to this treasured possession, to which everyone has a sort of "biological right." In the anti-psychiatric view, sanity is synonymous with an authentic or true self, which is also conceived of, in the Rousseauesque tradition, as a universal human possession or potentiality, and it, too, is achieved without personal effort; insanity results from damage to or loss of this treasured possession to which everyone has a sort of "political right." The former view presupposes "normal" brain development as a "natural" process; the latter, "normal" self-development. This pure and healthy brain/self is then pictured as destroyed or deformed by syphilization or civilization. Actually, as recently as two generations ago these two processes were said to go hand in hand. Syphilization has since dropped back as a major contender in the race for corrupting mankind, leaving civilization—at least among the anti-capitalists and anti-psychiatrists—undisputedly in the lead.

Clearly, both of these views contain a measure of truth; how large or small that measure is depends on time, place, and person. Syphilis does cause paresis. Parents, teachers, people in power can "cause" extreme human anguish and misery in those who depend on them, and do, in that sense, "drive people crazy." But what both of these models obscure are the simplest and most ancient of human truths; namely, that life is an arduous and tragic struggle; that what we call "sanity"—what we mean by "not being schizophrenic"—has a great deal to do with competence, earned by struggling for excellence; with compassion, hard won by confronting conflict; and with modesty and patience, acquired through silence and suffering. This image, not so much of some sort of idealistic sanity or mental health, but simply of being able to endure life with decency and dignity, cannot be fitted into the paradigms of either paresis or plunder. It requires an altogether different model or perspective— something like a sculptor carving a statue out of stone. There is no statue hidden in the stone. If a man with a piece of marble in his possession has no marble statue, it is not because his crusading enemy has smashed it because it is the wrong idol; nor because his colonizing conqueror has stolen it because he wants it for himself; but because he has failed to transform the stone into a statue.

The obligation to transform oneself from infant into child, adolescent, and adult (into whatever it is we think we ought to be), and the failure to meet this obligation—for reasons too numerous to consider here but clearly including the nature of that very "self" whose self-making is our concern—all this finds no place in the theories of either psychiatry or anti-psychiatry. Psychiatrists and anti-psychiatrists are equally simplistic in their causal imageries and remedial strategies. In the psychiatric view, medical research will make everyone sane. In the anti-psychiatric view, allowing incompetent, destructive, and self-destructive persons to wallow in their self-contempt and contempt of others will suffice to guide them safely through their journey in the Alps of alienation, after which all will arrive in the neat and clean Swiss village and live happily ever after. Such are the promises of the propagandists for psychiatric research on the one hand, and for anti-psychiatric retreats on the other.

Chapter 3

Schizophrenia: Psychiatric Syndrome or Scientific Scandal?

IF SIXTY-FIVE YEARS of "progress" in modern "scientific" psychiatry has accomplished anything, it has been to establish schizophrenia as an irrefutably real or genuine disease—or, as the psychiatric sophisticates would now have it, as a syndrome. And what is a syndrome? According to Webster, it is "A group of signs and symptoms that occur together and characterize a disease." In short, it is yet another psychosemantic trick to affirm that a "disease" without a demonstrable histopathological lesion or pathophysiological abnormality is nevertheless a disease.

Schizophrenia is defined so vaguely that, in actuality, it is a term often applied to almost any kind of behavior of which the speaker disapproves. It would therefore be as impossible to review the phenomenology of schizophrenia as it would be to review the phenomenology of heresy. It is possible, however, to review some characteristic modern writings about schizophrenia, illustrate the typical ways this term is used, and thus show that not only does it not identify any demonstrable disease, it does not even point to any objectively demonstrable referent. None of this means that the term is meaningless. On the contrary, its meaning is the more powerful because it is inscrutable. In short, I shall try to show that schizophrenia is a sacred symbol of psychiatry, in the same sort of sense in which, say, the crucified Christ is a sacred symbol of Christianity.

The entire literature on "schizophrenia"—now extending backward in time for nearly seventy years, and encompassing hundreds of thousands of "learned" books and essays in all the important languages—is, in my opinion, fatally flawed by a single logical error: namely, all of the contributions to it treat "schizophrenia" as if it were the shorthand *description* of a *disease,* when in fact it is the shorthand *prescription* of a disposition; in other words, they use the term *schizophrenia* as if it were a *proposition asserting* something about psychotics, when in fact it is a *justification legitimizing* something that *psychiatrists* do to them.

Professionals and laymen alike have thus come to believe that when psychiatrists speak of a person having or suffering from "schizophrenia," the term refers to a disease that is analogous, at least logically, to an injury, an infection, a metabolic disorder, or a tumor. This is simply not so. What such psychiatrists actually refer to is a complex set of moral and legal justifications for imprisoning such a "patient" and calling it "mental hospitalization." The relevant passages on the treatment of schizophrenia in any standard textbook on psychiatry support this interpretation.

Lawrence Kolb's phrasing of it, in his classic *Noyes' Modern Clinical Psychiatry,* is typical:

> Ideally, treatment of the schizophrenic should have begun before obvious symptoms of mental disorder are manifest. Unfortunately, this rarely occurs. The patient only occasionally seeks treatment himself. . . . Following the initial examination, decision must usually be made as to whether the patient should be treated in an outpatient department or office or admitted to a hospital. If behavior has been disturbed and promises to threaten later social acceptance, prompt admission for hospital treatment is indicated.[1]

The real facts of the matter are here so scrupulously avoided that it would not be too much to say that the author of this account is deliberately mendacious. If the schizophrenic does not "seek treatment himself," how does he ever come into the psychiatrist's presence? The answer is: usually someone brings him by force or fraud. Furthermore, if, as Kolb says, a "decision must . . . be made" about where the "patient" should be "treated," who is to make it? By not saying candidly and clearly that this decision is usually made by the so-called patient's relatives, by institutional psychiatrists, and by courts, Kolb makes it appear as if it were like any other medical decision, made cooperatively and jointly by a physician and his fully informed patient, who has an unqualified right to reject treatment.

In recent years, as increasing legal and popular attention has been directed toward psychiatric deprivations of human rights, psychiatrists have redoubled their effort simply to ignore the subject of psychiatric coercion whenever possible. Illustrative of the extremes to which such denial may go is Volume I of *The World Biennial of Psychiatry and Psychotherapy,* edited by Silvano Arieti.[2] In the index to this large volume, running to more than 600 pages and containing two chapters specifically on schizophrenia, one looks in vain for the terms *hospitalization, involuntary, coercion, compulsion,* or *commitment.* In the text, so far as I have been able to ascertain, there is not the remotest reference to the fact that psychiatrists lock up people, especially people called "schizophrenic." Yet, obscenely enough, the volume includes an entire chapter by A. V. Snezhnevsky, Director of the Institute of Psychiatry in Moscow and one of the most notorious of the Soviet medical criminals responsible for the psychiatric detention and destruction of dissidents.[3] Similarly, Ari Kiev, the editor of *Psychiatry in the Communist World,* as well as the numerous contributors to this volume, totally ignore involuntary psychiatry.[4] And so it goes.

Only a few years ago psychiatrists were more blatant and brazen in acknowledging that "schizophrenics" are, and indeed ought to be, locked up in insane asylums. In 1938, fresh out of

Germany, Franz Josef Kallmann—the pioneer geneticist of mental disorders—offered this revealing opinion about the connection between "schizophrenia" and loss of liberty:

> It is generally known that even today the commitment of many schizophrenics occurs tardily. The blame for the delay lies in the prejudice of the lay public against psychiatric institutions, as well as in the failure of some officials and physicians to understand the nature of schizophrenic psychoses. . . . The battle against these long-standing prejudices, which still oppose prompt hospitalization of the insane, must be an important point in any effective program of eugenics.[5]

Since "schizophrenia" is not a descriptive but a dispositive term—since it does not explain what is wrong with the alleged patient, but justifies what "his" psychiatrist does to him—it is, in my opinion, simply pointless to continue to treat the term as if it were the name of a disease whose biological character is exactly like that of any other "organic" disease. Nevertheless, according to the official—medical, psychiatric, legal, scientific —view, the proposition that schizophrenia is a disease is now a foregone conclusion. Hence, the loyal psychiatrist's task is not to speculate about whether schizophrenia is a disease, but to develop methods for its more accurate diagnosis and more effective treatment. The discovery of lobotomy exemplifies this orientation.

In 1935 Egas Moniz (1874–1955), a Portuguese neurologist and neurosurgeon, introduced prefrontal lobotomy into psychiatry, and in 1949 he received the Nobel Prize for it. The citation for his work read: "For his discovery of the therapeutic value of prefrontal leucotomy in certain psychoses." [7] Thus, explicitly, the lofty ceremonial of the Nobel award recognized Moniz as a great scientist and benefactor of mankind; implicitly, it recognized that "certain psychoses"—for the most part what American psychiatrists would diagnose as schizophrenia—were diseases due to an abnormal functioning of the brain. What else could justify so radical an operation on the human brain?

Here, in Moniz's own words, is his explanation of how lobotomy "cures," and his justification for performing this operation:

Starting from [the foregoing] anatomical facts I arrived at the conclusion that the synapses, which are found in billions of cells, are the organic foundation of thought. Normal psychic life depends upon the good functioning of the synapses and mental disorders appear as a result of synaptic derangements. . . . All of these considerations led me to the following conclusion: it is necessary to alter these synaptic adjustments and change the paths chosen by the impulses in their constant passage so as to modify the corresponding ideas and force thought into different channels.[8]

It is interesting and ironic that the identification of thoughts with synapses offered by Moniz, the validity of which was implicitly authenticated by his work being rewarded with a Nobel Prize, is of exactly the same sort as the identification of the body of Jesus with its literal presence in the Eucharist, the validity of which is authenticated by the Catholic doctrine of transubstantiation.[9] As the latter identification could not be doubted or challenged in the Age of Faith, so the former cannot be doubted or challenged in the Age of Science. Furthermore, as priests, under the authority of the Inquisition, used the rack and the stake to "force thought into different channels," so physicians, under the authority of Medicine, use lobotomy and other methods of psychiatric torture to effect the same ends. Revealingly, prefrontal lobotomy for "mental illness" is, so far as I know, the only "medical treatment" that has been formally condemned by the Vatican and banned in the Soviet Union.

More revealingly still, Moniz acknowledges that his aim in trying out lobotomy on human beings was not so much to find a cure for "psychosis" as to find support for the ideological cornerstone of "organic psychiatry"—that is, to establish a firm foundation for "the study of the psychic functions on an organic basis":

> On the eve of my first attempt, in my justified anxiety at that moment, all fears were swept aside by the hope of obtaining favorable results. If we could suppress certain symptomatic complexes of psychic nature by destroying the cell-connecting groups, we would prove definitely that the psychic functions and the brain areas which contributed to their elaboration were closely related. That would be a great step forward as a fundamental fact in the study of the psychic functions on an organic basis.[10]

I cite Moniz's work not so much to condemn it as to underscore the fundamental departure, in this type of investigation, from traditional methods of medical research. To establish the organic nature of paresis, medical investigators studied the brains of dead paretics and sought to define and demonstrate the histopathology of the disease. They did not try to prove that paresis was an organic brain disease by mutilating the paretic's body, calling it "treatment," and making inferences from the "therapeutic" intervention to the nature of the disease. However, lobotomy, as well as insulin shock before it and electroshock after it, were introduced into psychiatry, and their use was justified, on the basis of just such a perversion of logic and of the scientific method. The reasoning behind, and the results of, this method of "research" are now widely accepted. For example, it is widely believed that because so-called major tranquilizers affect so-called psychotic behavior in ways that many people consider to be desirable, this "proves" that the "patients" so "treated" suffer from a "mental disease" which has an "organic basis."

Thus, while the more romantic and radical therapies of schizophrenia come and go, the psychopharmacologists are now settling down in earnest to work for all its worth their particular vein of this taxpayer-funded goldmine. Consider in this connection an announcement in the March 1975 issue of the magazine *Current Prescribing*. Under the heading "What's New," subtitled "A monthly round of new drugs, new drugs-to-be, and new uses for old drugs," three new drugs are described: "Carbazepine for seizures," "Glyburide, an investigational sulfonylurea," and "Molindone HCl in schizophrenia. Molindone (Moban, Endo) has recently been marketed for the treatment of acute and chronic schizophrenia." There follows a description of its dosage, adverse effects, metabolism, and, finally, "Evaluation: Molindone is as effective in schizophrenia as currently used drugs, and offers an alternative in refractory patients." [11]

If a physician reads enough of this sort of stuff, he might easily come to believe that schizophrenia is a disease, "like any other." Thus, he would "know" that schizophrenia is a disease, although he could never be quite sure that the patient he is treating for it has really got it. This situation, so typical of contemporary "psychiatric medicine," completes the conquest of real (organic) medicine by fake (psychiatric) medicine: in the old days, physicians diagnosed diseases which they could not treat; now they treat diseases which they cannot diagnose.

A recent essay by a leading British psychiatrist lends further support to my contention that schizophrenia is the sacred symbol of psychiatry, and that it constitutes the ground on which psychiatrists, besieged by an enemy ever more vigorously and successfully unmasking their medical pretensions and moral depredations, are now regrouping for a new defense of their homeland, or perhaps for launching a fresh counteroffensive. In a thoughtful article, R. E. Kendell, Professor of Psychiatry at the University of Edinburgh, sounds the trumpet for the strategic retreat of psychiatry.[12] He candidly acknowledges that disagreement is not disease, and that psychiatrists have claimed too large a territory for themselves.

The enemy, in this imagery, is my criticism of the medical claims for, and conceptualization of, so-called mental illnesses, which is attracting increasing support in various circles. The American Psychiatric Association has, of course, already retreated from one of its exposed flanks by abandoning its claims to homosexuality as a disease.[13] Kendell counsels abandoning all of the occupied and outlying territories and taking up positions in the heavily fortified capital:

> It is worth reflecting whether the many attempts we have recently witnessed to discredit the concept of mental illness might not be a reaction to the equally absurd claims we have made that all unhappiness and all undesirable behaviour are manifestations of mental illness.[14]

Kendell seems ready to concede that not only homosexuality but also anxieties and obsessions, fears and depressions, and all the myriad things listed in psychiatric textbooks as mental diseases are, in fact, nothing of the sort. Surely this admission on the part of so respected a psychiatric authority is powerful evidence that concealed behind the screen of "mental illness" lies a twentieth-century scientific scandal of the first order. Kendell's retreat to the stronghold of schizophrenia—a fortress he thinks is secure—is equally self-incriminating: "By all means let us insist," he concludes, but without offering any evidence for his conclusion, "that schizophrenia is an illness and that we are better equipped to understand and treat it than anyone else. But let us not try to do the same for all the woes of mankind." [15]

Certainly, prominent psychiatrists, as loyal members of their guild and patriotic leaders of their fellow members, are entitled, are indeed expected, to make such claims. But the issue is not whether psychiatrists "understand" schizophrenia better than do other people. It is whether schizophrenia is a disease like paresis or pellagra, and whether psychiatrists should be deputized by the state to confine persons diagnosed as "having" it.

Actually, neither Kendell, nor Moniz, nor anyone else has demonstrated the validity of these two crucial propositions—one medical and scientific, the other moral and political—on which the claims of modern psychiatrists concerning schizophrenia and their conduct toward schizophrenics rest. That is to say, no one has demonstrated that the alleged clinical syndrome called "schizophrenia" is consistently correlated with histopathological lesions in the brains of schizophrenics, and only of schizophrenics. Or that alleged "schizophrenics" (and perhaps some other "psychotics") are dangerous to themselves or others; that persons belonging to other classes of human beings are not equally or even more dangerous to themselves or others; that the measures imposed involuntarily on "schizophrenics" do in fact render them less dangerous to themselves or others; and that, for these reasons, the use of involuntary psychiatric interventions, such as have traditionally and typically been imposed on "schizophrenics," is morally and politically justified. On this last issue—of "schizophrenia" as justificatory rhetoric legitimizing involuntary psychiatric interventions—Kendell, too, remains revealingly silent.

In effect, then, the medical perspective on schizophrenia is a call to arms: it is a command to deny both what so-called schizophrenics do, and what physicians do to them; and instead to insist that what the "psychotics" do are the symptoms of a disease for which they are not responsible, and what the institutional psychiatrists do are investigations into the nature and treatments of a disease for which they are responsible and for which they deserve humanity's boundless gratitude. I shall now try to offer evidence to support this view.

In a paper published in the *American Journal of Psychiatry,* the official organ of the American Psychiatric Association, Albert Urmer, of the University of California at Los Angeles, reviews the implications of California's new mental health law.[16] This law, known as the Lanterman-Petris-Short (LPS) Act, went into effect in 1969, and made psychiatric commitment much more difficult than it had been theretofore. Remarking on the consequences of this act, the author, by no means an opponent of coercive psychiatry, casually notes:

> Experience with California's new law has also shown that the mental health system is frequently used to house socially incompetent individuals and that alternative systems are developed when this system becomes unavailable. For example, a significant proportion of individuals had been committed to state hospitals before LPS, not because they were violent or suicidal but because they were a nuisance to society. . . .[17]

This phrase, "because they were a nuisance to society," will serve as our point of departure for much of what follows. Of course, everyone in psychiatry, and many people outside of it, know and always have known that this is really the reason why people get locked up in mental hospitals: because they are a nuisance. But this idea or phrase does not appear in the most recent version of the *Diagnostic and Statistical Manual* of the American Psychiatric Association,[18] which lists the mental diseases officially recognized by this learned body. How, then, were these persons—who, according to Urmer, were hospitalized only because they were nuisances—classified? Since 25 percent of the patients in United States public mental hospitals are admitted as schizophrenics and since 60 percent of those now residing in such hospitals are so classified,[19] we can safely assume that at least one-quarter of the patients Urmer refers to was diagnosed as schizophrenic.

I have documented elsewhere which troublemakers get called "schizophrenic" by which authorities, why, and how they are then hospitalized and treated for this "illness"; [20] I shall add to this documentation, especially as concerns the use of this diagnosis in Soviet Russia, presently. Before doing so, however, I want to call attention to a recent California Department of Mental Hygiene Study which confirms conclusively my contention that many so-called patients "diagnosed" and "treated" by institutional psychiatrists are actually medically healthy persons who are regarded as patients solely because they reside in a state mental institution.[21] Discussing the mortality rates of several different groups in a geriatric mental hospital population, the authors of this study identify the two groups with the lowest mortality rate as the "elite patients" and the "normal patients." Greenblatt and Glazier—who cite this study with unbounded approval, completely oblivious of the moral and political implications of classifying people as "normal patients"—identify the two groups as follows:

> "Elite" patients were described as highly sociable and responsive, independent in self-care, and physically healthy but manifesting a relatively large number of psychiatric symptoms. "Normal" patients were described as not debilitated in any sphere, as alert, responsive, physically healthy, and without psychiatric symptoms.[22]

The latter group is actually "healthier" than the "healthy population," as that population is described by psychiatric epidemiologists and madness-mongers.[23] Despite such a crass admission that many of the people confined in state mental hospitals are "healthy," the pious pretense that such institutions serve the aim of "treating sick patients" for their "mental diseases" continues unabated—and is now powerfully reinforced not only by the claims of psychiatric inquisitors preaching a "right to treatment," but also by the contentions of civil rights lawyers and "liberal" jurists reinterpreting the Constitution so as to give the inquisitors a "right to treat" their victims.[24]

The proposition that the real meaning of schizophrenia has always been, and continues to be, "crazy" and therefore "committable," is supported by the widespread use of this "diagnosis" in Soviet Russia. If the Russian authorities had only wanted to demean and insult their dissidents, they and their psychiatric lackeys could have pinned any derogatory psychiatric diagnosis on them. They could have called them manics or obsessionals or homosexuals. Why, then, did they choose to call them schizophrenics? Because, more than any other psychiatric diagnostic term, *schizophrenia* carries with it the implication that the person so "diagnosed" is crazy, does not know what he is doing, is not responsible for his behavior, and should be so "treated." This explains why *schizophrenia* has justified, and continues to justify, the imposition of involuntary psychiatric interventions on the "patient" so diagnosed.

While an adequate presentation and discussion of Soviet barbarities justified by appeals to "schizophrenia" would require a book, I want to offer a few remarks to illustrate the actual, as against the abstract, meaning and use of this term. The following quotations are from an interview with a Russian psychiatrist, Dr. Marina Woikhanskaya,[25] who identifies herself as follows:

I left the Soviet Union on the 11th April, 1975, and in the Soviet Union I have been working as a psychiatrist for the last 12 years. I worked in one of the largest city hospitals. I was very fond of my patients and very proud of my work for it was one of the most humane types of work that could exist.[26]

In 1974 she at last realizes that the situation is not quite so idyllic. But of course she still loves the system: "I learned that in various hospitals in the Soviet Union there are quite a number of so-called dissidents." Schizophrenics, however, are never "so-called" to Woikhanskaya. They are "real." She believes in schizophrenia as firmly as she believes in Marxism. "This problem [i.e., the "abuse" of psychiatry] worries me greatly," she says, "and it worries honest Soviet psychiatrists greatly." [27] What "honest psychiatrists" actually do in the Soviet Union we soon learn, all too clearly, from her answers to the interviewer's pointed questions:

Question. How frequently in general psychiatric cases, that's apart from the dissidents, is compulsory treatment undertaken in the Soviet Union?

Woikhanskaya. A mentally ill person has no rights in the Soviet Union and it is entirely the decision of the doctors to send this person to hospital or not, and if the doctor thinks that there is any danger of this person behaving in an unpermissible way, to hospital this person goes.

Question. And that applies to all psychiatric cases?

Woikhanskaya. Yes.[28]

Then we learn about schizophrenia in Russia, and realize, if only we are willing to face it, how little this "disease" has changed from Bleuler's Zürich to Brezhnev's Moscow:

Question. If the dissidents are admitted officially, there must be some official diagnostic category which they come under and there must be criteria which they have to fit in order to be admitted in this way?

Woikhanskaya. The diagnosis is of a boring and consistent type. Slow Schizophrenia, Reforming Syndrome, Chronic Schizophrenia, Creeping or Smouldering Schizophrenia, and Syndrome of Reform Seeking Schizophrenic types. . . . They are given insulin treatment, they are given E.C.T. treatment. They are not ill, but the treatment, yes, is the standard one for ill people.[29]

Here it is, all of it, in pure culture: "Seeking reform" as "schizophrenia"; the psychiatric incarceration of the "patient"; and his involuntary "treatment." If linguistic philosophers and semanticists are right in insisting that what a word means must be inferred from the way it is used, then this is what *schizophrenia* means—not just in Communist Russia but everywhere.

A brief case history of the "diagnosis" and "treatment" of a "dissident" was published in a recent issue of the *New Statesman*.[30] It complements and amplifies Dr. Woikhanskaya's account.

A young man, Jan Krilsky, a Jew and a Zionist, is arrested in the USSR for entering a factory illegally, with a friend's pass. The police ask: Who would he fight for in the event of war between Israel and Russia? Israel, he answers. Here is what happened next:

His father, called by the KGB, agreed to his son's committal to Jaroslavl [a city near Moscow] mental hospital for treatment for schizophrenia, but only, he claims, in desperation to avoid a long prison sentence. (Jan was now 18.) The treatment was of course injections of sulphazine, purified sulphur in peach kernel oil, which sent his temperature soaring to 41C (105.8 F). There is no modern use for the drug, according to Dr. Harold Merskey, a London psychiatrist and chairman of the Medical and Scientific Committee for Soviet Jewry. . . . The boy was moved to the Yakovenko closed mental hospital in Moscow and six months later released as "well" by a commission of doctors. . . . [Later], while he was under arrest, the KGB drafted a letter to Foreign Minister Gromyko about his desire to go to Israel, and Jan signed angrily. This was tantamount to a confession of madness. In the space of a few weeks, he was shunted from one hospital to another.[31]

Receiving these free benefits of the Russian health care system was evidently enough to make even Jan's father, who had been a loyal Communist Party member for fifty-two years, see the light:

By now, Julius, the father, had had enough. He submitted an official request for the family to be allowed to emigrate to Israel. . . . [Whereupon an old criminal charge against him was reopened, and the court] committed Jan to a mental hospital "until he recovers from militant Zionism." [32]

However glaring these "psychiatric abuses" may seem, the concepts and methods of the Russian psychiatric gangsters who perpetrate them are legitimized and supported by their colleagues in the West. Even Kendell, now the acknowledged dean of British psychodiagnosticians, shies away from criticizing them! In his recent, comprehensive book, *The Role of Diagnosis in Psychiatry,* where he never mentions the psychiatric repression of deviants in Russia or elsewhere, he states:

The Russian concept of this illness [schizophrenia] embraces three sub-types, periodic, sluggish, and shift-like schizophrenia, which are not recognized elsewhere. In general, Russian psychiatrists appear to be influenced more by the course of the illness and less by its actual symptomatology than other European psychiatrists, a fact which has some bearing on recent political controversies.[33]

The Russian psychiatrists who make and support such diagnoses of schizophrenia on "dissidents" are, of course, members of the same international psychiatric organizations as are Western psychiatrists—and as are the American psychiatrists who make and support the diagnoses of schizophrenia on "madmen" like Ezra Pound and James Forrestal. "Patients" like these form the "clinical" base on which other "researchers" rest their theories about the nature and cause of schizophrenia, and their recommendations for its proper treatment.

Let us now consider how this simple factual problem—namely, that people get locked up in mental hospitals because they annoy others and are then called "schizophrenic"—may affect the validity of the pronouncements of some of the most famous contemporary biologists, chemists, and geneticists.

In 1970, geneticist Dr. Joshua Lederberg, a Nobel Prize winner in medicine and physiology

> asked for the establishment of a national task force on genetic research to help bring to realization a new era in medicine. He urged that Congress appropriate an additional $10 million for the coming fiscal year to further genetic research. . . . Dr. Lederberg said that diseases known to be of wholly genetic origin made up only about one-quarter of the total, but there were many major diseases in which hereditary factors were believed to play some part. Among those he listed diabetes and schizophrenia.[34]

But how would Lederberg know that someone has schizophrenia? We may assume that he would not make the diagnosis himself, but would rely on a reputable psychiatrist to make it. He would thus base his genetic speculation on a professionally organized and supported fraud—whose fraudulence he accepts rather than scrutinizes.

The foregoing example—a biologist basing his work on the premise of a medically established diagnosis of schizophrenia— is characteristic of a great deal of the genetic literature on schizophrenia. For example, Sir Julian Huxley, one of the foremost biologists of our day, has asserted that "It now appears clear that schizophrenia, at least in the great majority of cases, is based on a single partially dominant gene with low penetrance. We wish to put forward the hypothesis that it involves a genetic morphism. . . ." [35] One wonders whose schizophrenia Huxley has in mind—Jesus's? Lincoln's? Hitler's? Stalin's? All these men, and of course countless others less well known, have been diagnosed as schizophrenic—by experts Huxley presumably respects and trusts.

Considering the way schizophrenia is diagnosed, it is remarkable how much space prestigious scientific journals give to the repeated declarations of researchers that schizophrenia is, first, a disease, and second, a genetic disease. In 1970 *Science* published one of its periodic reaffirmations of the reality of the disease concept of schizophrenia. In it Leonard Heston, a psychiatrist, asserted:

> The contribution of genetic factors to the etiology of schizophrenia has been confirmed decisively. . . . The importance of genetic factors in the development of schizophrenia has by now been established beyond reasonable dispute. . . . From the known risk of schizophrenia for the population as a whole, it is estimated that at least 4 percent of the general population will be afflicted with schizoid-schizophrenic disease.[36]

This is doubly reassuring to psychiatry: it guarantees it a secure supply of patients, and brands all views skeptical of those here affirmed as "unreasonable."

In the same year Elaine Cumming, a sociologist then working as one of the chief ceremonialists for the New York State Department of Mental Hygiene, wrote a guest editorial for the *American Journal of Psychiatry*. After a page and a half of platitudes comes this remarkable conclusion:

> Above all, in psychiatry we have the extra problem of the stigma still attached to our illnesses. Half our research seems to have a subtle goal of somehow "placing the blame" for such personally and socially undermining illness as schizophrenia. Such a frame of mind is debilitating to enquiry, although perhaps necessary for our social survival. At any rate, discovery of a virus or a replaceable biochemical link in the causal chain [of schizophrenia] would be a double deliverance, for epidemiologists as well as from a truly awful illness.[37]

This is a wonderfully revealing conclusion from a researcher who, I suspect, really knew better. If, as she says, schizophrenia were an illness, that would indeed be a "deliverance" for psychiatry. From what? From the fraud of being a fake medical specialty. It would certainly be a deliverance for psychiatry if schizophrenia could be shown to be due to a virus or a genetic defect. It would, I dare say, also please capitalists if communism could be shown to be such a "mental illness," and vice versa. It would also please Jews if Mohammedanism could be shown to be a "mental illness," and vice versa. In other words, in our medically intoxicated world it is generally believed that in a disagreement between two parties, if one could show that the other is "sick"—especially "schizophrenic"—this would irrefutably establish the superiority, at once scientific and moral, of the former over the latter. How else can we explain the fervent hope, in virtually all "scientific" circles, that schizophrenia is a disease, preferably a genetic disease? Why is there not also hope in such quarters that it is a myth, a medical mistake made and mandated by the desire to confine certain troublemakers? Might that not also help the victims?

The standard British rhetoric about schizophrenia is indistinguishable from the American. In an editorial in the *New Scientist* we are informed:

> Schizophrenia is a ghastly disease afflicting one in a hundred of the population and blighting the lives of many more through the effect that the schizophrenic can have on the rest of his or her family. Some 60,000 of the hospital beds in Britain are occupied by schizophrenics. . . . All this occurs against a scientific background of overwhelming evidence pointing to the disease having a genetic basis, probably mediated through biochemical changes in the brain. It is not mystical; it has physical causes; and is—given enough fundamental research—curable.[38]

I dare say that never in the history of modern medicine have so many authorities made so many assertions about the cause of a disease where the disease in question could not even be objectively identified by means of histopathological or pathophysiological criteria and observations; where, in other words, the very identity, not to mention the nature, of the disease which the authorities so self-assuredly, indeed arrogantly, set out to research and cure is shrouded, if not in mystery, then surely in controversy.

There is at present no demonstrable histopathological or pathophysiological evidence to support the claim that schizophrenia is a disease. Indeed, if there were any, the supporters of this claim would be the first to assert that schizophrenia is not a mental disease but a brain disease. Nevertheless, according to current psychiatric doctrine, honored the world over, schizophrenia is a disease; it is, moreover, "basically" the same everywhere, although, because of differences in national life styles, psychiatrists in different countries tend to diagnose it somewhat differently.

Dr. Steven R. Hirsch, senior lecturer at Westminster Hospital in London, thus reports that American psychiatrists make the diagnosis of schizophrenia twice as often as do British psychiatrists.[39]

Dr. Tolani Asuni, director of the Neuropsychiatric Hospital, Aro-Abeokuta, in Nigeria, declares that "Schizophrenia cannot be the exclusive product of Western society because it accounts for 70 percent of the admissions to African psychiatric hospitals." [40]

Dr. Jimmie Holland, of the Albert Einstein College of Medicine, relates, on the basis of her personal experiences in the USSR, that "Once a patient in the Soviet Union is diagnosed as having schizophrenia, he is considered always to be schizophrenic even though he may become asymptomatic." [41] She remarks:

> Soviet psychiatrists found it hard to believe that not all American hippies are schizophrenic. . . . A Soviet psychiatrist may sincerely believe that a political dissenter has the continuous form of schizophrenia, because a dissenter would appear to have overvalued ideas of his own importance and of the correctness of his ideological views on political change. . . . Patients have no choice about the psychiatrist who treats them. . . . The psychiatrist's behavior is kindly, concerned, paternal, and strongly authoritarian. He has the power to change the patient's job situation, place him on leave, and make other decisions about his life. . . .[42]

Lest it be thought that only the contemporary definitions and uses of schizophrenia are so loose, variable, and morally judgmental—that the diagnosis was defined and used more carefully and narrowly in the past—I shall cite an example to dispel this belief. Its source is again Kallmann who, it must be remembered, is considered to be the founding father of modern psychiatric genetics. Among the patients he reported in his classic study of 1,087 schizophrenics, he included a "subgroup" which he called "schizoid psychopaths," and whose members he described as follows:

> In classifying the schizoid psychopaths, we again interpreted the diagnosis as strictly as possible [*sic*]. . . . Our concept of schizoid psychopath therefore embraces the unsociable, cold-hearted, indecisive and fanatic types regarded by Schneider as prototypes of the catatoid, heboid, schizoid, and paranoid cases, respectively, as well as Hoffmann's bull-headed oafs, malicious tyrants, queer cranks, overpedantic schemers, prudish "model children," and daydreamers out of all touch with reality. However, we included only psychopathic individuals who showed the fundamental schizoid characteristics of autistic introversion, emotional inadequacy, sudden surges of temperament and inappropriate motor response to emotional stimuli, and in whom such symptoms of schizoid abnormality as bigotry, pietism, avarice, superstition, suspicion, obstinacy or crankiness were present to a striking and disproportionate degree, dominating the personality of the individuals in question.[43]

Is this an account of what Kendell claims is an unquestionably bona fide medical disease? Or of the "symptoms" of such a disease? If the term *schizophrenia* did not conceal so immense a human problem one might be tempted to stop right here. For what more evidence is needed to show what a cruel hoax it all is? That schizophrenia is not a scientific hypothesis but a sacred symbol? And that, as such—like the medieval Host stabbed by malicious Jews—it displays the most terrifying "symptoms" and hence justifies the most merciless measures? [44]

The examples I have cited—and there are countless others

just like them—illustrate two things. First, that none of the experts cited seems to have the least doubt that schizophrenia is a disease which he knows how to recognize and identify. Second, that there is confusion—in the minds of these experts, in their accounts, and in psychiatry generally—about the differences between science and politics, between medical diagnosis as technical taxonomy and psychiatric diagnosis as political action. Scientific propositions are supported by evidence: for example, the proposition that paresis is a syphilitic infection of the brain is buttressed by the evidence of Treponema pallida in the brains of such patients. Political actions, on the other hand, are supported not by evidence but by power: for example, the policy of forcibly confining certain people without accusing them of crime or trying them for it, and of forcibly imposing the stigmatizing label "schizophrenia" on them, is buttressed not by any evidence of morphological lesions in their brain, but by the power of the authorities to act in these particular ways toward these particular persons. The use of such power is clear, and is not usually contested, when the forcible imposition of stigmatized role and confined status is carried out without the participation of medical or psychiatric personnel. For example, when the Nazis stigmatize and segregate Jews, that is persecution; when the Americans stigmatize and segregate their fellow Americans who have black skin or Japanese ancestry, that is also persecution. But when people throughout the world stigmatize and segregate their relatives and neighbors who behave in ways which the majority do not like —and when that stigmatization is carried out by means of pseudomedical stigmata and pseudomedical segregations—then it is generally accepted not as persecution, but psychiatry.[45]

While some experts worry about the nature and cause of schizophrenia, others—among them biologists and chemists as well as psychiatrists—are ready to treat it. Among the nonpsychiatrists offering a cure for it is no less an authority than Linus Pauling, recipient of two Nobel Prizes. As coeditor of a book titled *Orthomolecular Psychiatry,* and modestly subtitled *Treatment of Schizophrenia,* Pauling claims that schizophrenia is curable with "megavitamin therapy," that is, with massive doses of vitamins.[46] How he knows that he is treating a bona fide case of schizophrenia is unclear. We must assume that Pauling accepts his psychiatric colleagues' dictum that what they *call* schizophrenia *is* schizophrenia—a posture that ill becomes a scientist of his stature.

In his preface to *Orthomolecular Psychiatry,* Pauling writes:

> In the article *Insanity* in the ninth edition of the Encyclopaedia Britannica (1881), insanity is defined as a chronic disease of the brain inducing chronic disordered mental symptoms. The author of the article (J. Batty Tuke, M.D., Lecturer on Insanity, School of Medicine, Edinburgh) then stated that this definition possesses the great practical advantage of keeping before the student the primary fact that insanity is the result of disease of the brain. . . . At the present day . . . it is universally accepted that the brain is the organ through which mental phenomena are manifested, and therefore that it is impossible to conceive of the existence of an insane mind in a healthy brain.[47]

Pauling quotes this passage, articulating the paradigm of the paretic mind, with unqualified approval. But while Tuke asserts a hypothesis, Pauling treats it as if it were a fact. Interestingly, Pauling does not attempt to prove that schizophrenia is a brain disease, as Noguchi and Moore proved that paresis was, but tries to establish the validity of his claim by citing, and rejecting, the Freudian claim that "mental disease" is "psychogenic":

> By 1929, when the fourteenth edition of the Encyclopaedia Britannica was published, the situation had changed, largely

because of the development of psychoanalysis by Sigmund Freud. The earlier definition of insanity was deleted, and replaced by discussions from two points of view [one organic, the other psychogenic].[48]

After quoting the standard psychoanalytic definition of "mental disease," but without remarking on the change of terminology from "insanity" to "mental disease," Pauling continues as follows:

Psychoanalysis has failed, and psychiatry is now rapidly returning to the scientific approach, the recognition of the corporeal character of mental disease. . . . The recognition of the effectiveness of phenothiazines and other drugs (and the ineffectiveness of psychoanalysis) has accelerated the reacceptance of the concept that mental disease is disease of the brain, and that the brain itself needs to be treated, by changing its molecular composition.[49]

Pauling is saying several things here, all at once. We must untangle them and deal with each idea separately. First, Pauling seems to be saying that there is no mental illness, that there can be no mental illness, that illness is, by definition, bodily. With this I heartily agree. But if all so-called mental disease is brain disease, if all mental disease is really only the "mental symptom" of conditions such as paresis or pellagra—then it makes no sense to have two classes of brain diseases: one neurological, the other mental. Instead, it would be necessary to insist—as I have insisted—first, that brain diseases are brain diseases, and that mental diseases are not diseases at all; second, that a suspected brain disease does not become an actual brain disease until it is so proved by appropriate and consistently repeatable histopathological or pathophysiological findings; and third, that persons with or without brain diseases are "patients" only insofar as they consent to assuming that role—because as individuals in a free society they have a fundamental right to reject medical diagnosis, hospitalization, and treatment.

But these are not the inferences Pauling draws from his unsupported, and unsupportable, claim that all mental patients have brain diseases. Instead, Pauling draws three other inferences, all of which seem to me empty, false, or immoral. First, Pauling asserts that psychoanalysis has failed as a therapy; it has, but not because of the reasons he gives, but rather because conversation cannot cure real diseases, and because it is impossible to cure nonexisting ("mental") diseases.[50] Second, Pauling points to the use of modern psychopharmacologicals as evidence that mental diseases are brain diseases; he might as well point to the widespread use of alcohol or tobacco as evidence that a large proportion of the human race suffers from alcohol or nicotine deficiency. And third, Pauling declares that the "brain itself needs to be treated"; this is sloppy English, as brains, or livers, cannot be treated—only persons, or patients, can. In other words, Pauling evades the problem of whether the person who happens to be the unlucky owner of such a supposedly diseased brain should or should not have a say about its treatment. Pauling's evasion surely implies, and the psychiatric company he keeps implies decisively, that he favors treating such persons with their consent where consent can be secured, and treating them without their consent where it cannot (presumably obtaining consent from relatives or the courts, as is customary in pediatrics and psychiatry).

The upshot is that in Pauling's hands, or mind, there are, somehow, no psychiatric patients as persons or agents; there are only diseased brains needing fixing by orthomolecular treatment. His following statement, verging on the bizarre in its image of what psychotherapists do with their patients, strongly supports my foregoing remark:

The decision by most psychiatrists who do not accept the principles of orthomolecular psychiatry to restrict the intake of vitamins by their patients to certain arbitrary levels, without checking the possible benefit for the patient of an increased intake, cannot be justified.[51]

Psychiatrists, psychotherapists, and psychoanalysts have been accused of all sorts of mischief, even by me, but I dare say the accusation that they "restrict the intake of vitamins by their patients" is a new one. Pauling's choice of the word "decision" to describe "most psychiatrists' " control over their patients' vitamin intake is odd, to say the least. Actually, most psychiatrists do not know or care how many or how few vitamins their patients take; if Pauling does not know this, one wonders what, if anything, he knows about what goes on in psychiatry.[52]

I have commented on orthomolecular psychiatry in some detail, first, because of the exceptional eminence of its chief theoretician, Linus Pauling; second, because although Pauling and his followers claim that mental diseases are brain diseases, they nevertheless insist on calling them mental diseases; and third, because despite Pauling's fame as a civil libertarian, there is in the 697 pages of *Orthomolecular Psychiatry* not a single reference to the legal status of schizophrenics or other mental patients, to involuntary psychiatric interventions, or to any other civil rights aspect of psychiatric diagnosis, hospitalization, and treatment.

Long before Pauling lent the prestige of his name to their effort, Abram Hoffer and Humphry Osmond, two psychiatrists, had claimed that they could cure schizophrenia with vitamins and, curiously enough, with a self-help organization called Schizophrenics Anonymous International. Hoffer and Osmond set forth their views on schizophrenia in a pamphlet titled *What You Should Know About Schizophrenia,* issued by the American Schizophrenia Foundation, which is a nonprofit corporation they "own." In the acknowledgements to the brochure we are told that "This booklet was prepared by a recovered schizophrenic with the assistance of Dr. Abram Hoffer, director of psychiatric research, University Hospital, Saskatoon, Canada, and of Dr. Humphry Osmond, director, Bureau of Research in Neurology and Psychiatry, Princeton, N.J." [53] According to Hoffer and Osmond:

> Schizophrenia is not a way of life. It is not a crime. It does not favor artists or intellectuals. . . . It is not caused by devils or difficult mothers or tyrannical fathers or latent homosexuality or stress. . . . Schizophrenia is a physical *disease,* in the same way that pellagra and diabetes and mental retardation are physical diseases. And it is a disease which is the same in every part of the world.[54]

How do Hoffer and Osmond know this? Science tells them so:

> A large body of scientific evidence has recently been assembled indicating that the schizophrenic is a victim of a "metabolic error" in the chemistry of his body. This defect, probably inherited, causes the production of a poisonous substance that affects his brain and creates marked disturbance in perception and radical changes in thought, personality, and behavior.[55]

The fourteen-page pamphlet offers much interesting information, including a list of fourteen "warning signs of an approaching schizophrenic episode," the first four of which are: "1. Insomnia. 2. Headaches. 3. A change in skin color to a darker hue. 4. An ever-present offensive body odor. . . ." [56] It also includes injunctions such as "You must at all times rely on the judgment of your physician and follow his instructions faithfully." [57] There is no mention of the therapeutic effects of various brands of perfume on the offensive body odor of schizophrenics, nor of the social consequences of deodorizing them by commitment.

In addition to vitamins, Hoffer and Osmond also rely for their therapy on Schizophrenics Anonymous International, which they founded. According to an article in *The National Observer:*

> Any individual who has been diagnosed as a schizophrenic by a mental health specialist is invited to attend. Members recite the 12-step plan of "permanent hope," which includes a pledge of faith in God and a promise to follow prescribed medicine.[58]

The rules of Schizophrenics Anonymous International, as set forth in the organization's own pamphlet, require members to declare that they:

> Came to believe that a power greater than ourselves could restore us to sanity.
> Made a decision to turn our will and our lives over to the care of God as we understood Him. . . .
> Sought through prayer and meditation to improve our conscious contact with God . . . praying only for knowledge of His will for us and the power to carry that out.[59]

It would be hard to top Hoffer and Osmond's claims for sheer arrogance. Schizophrenia, they insist, is a physical disease just like pellagra and diabetes (the examples are theirs). Yet they recommend that persons afflicted with it "turn [their] will and [their] lives over to the care of God"—and Schizophrenics International. If this is not pure quackery, it would be difficult to know what is. In this connection, it is especially amusing to contemplate the unqualified support of Linus Pauling, the atheistic scientist, for this form of state-supported religion.

Many contemporary psychiatrists recognize, and acknowledge, that the referent to which the term *schizophrenia* points is uncertain and variable. But this in no way shakes their faith either in the reality of schizophrenia as a "disease" or in the medical and moral legitimacy of the term as a "diagnosis." The following remarks by the editors of the National Institute of Mental Health's *Schizophrenia Bulletin* are typical of this hypocrisy—that is, of admitting the weaknesses of a particular psychiatric diagnostic term only the better to justify its continued use for controlling deviance:

> What is or is not schizophrenia has been the subject of heated, if not illuminating, discussion ever since the term was coined by Bleuler in 1911. The fact that this diagnostic category has become widely accepted and used, even in the absence of a universally accepted definition, is remarkable. The ways in which the term "schizophrenia" has been applied vary widely and have been shown to be affected by such nonspecific (i.e., not patient-related) factors as the diagnostician's theoretical background and training, the nature of the relationship established in the diagnostic interview, and the context within which the interview is conducted (e.g. hospital or clinic). . . . And then, of course, there is the most difficult problem of all—it is not possible to validate a diagnosis of schizophrenia. There is no test which can independently confirm that the individual so designated is, in fact, schizophrenic.[60]

What these observers point out has, of course, always been known. The diagnosis of schizophrenia can no more be validated than can the "diagnosis" of "un-Americanism"—for the simple reason that neither is a medical diagnosis. It is utterly misleading to call the observations reported above "the most difficult problem" concerning schizophrenia: they are not "problems" at all, merely observations that themselves help to solve the so-called problem of schizophrenia by strongly suggesting that "schizophrenia" has never been, is not now, and probably never will be a bona fide medical diagnostic term.

However, none of this evidence prevents the editors of the *Schizophrenia Bulletin* from regarding schizophrenia as a medical disease. Nor does any of it deter the pushers of megavitamins from treating "schizophrenics" as if their disease were, in principle, no different from diabetes.[61]

This is not surprising. The diagnosis of schizophrenia was never intended to help the "patient." Why should we expect it to help him now? But the diagnosis helped Bleuler—it made him famous. And it does help contemporary psychiatrists to conceal their coercive meddling as "treatment."

I want to add here a brief observation on the relations between scientific knowledge about the nature of disease and medical claims about its treatment. Throughout the long history of medicine, the more uncertain has been the nature of a disease, the more numerous have been the treatments for it. Today there is surely no "disease" for which this is more true than for schizophrenia. There is no agreement on what schizophrenia is, or who really is or is not schizophrenic. And if the phenomenology of schizophrenia is hidden behind opaque windows, its etiology lies buried in utter darkness. None of this prevents physicians and medical scientists from continually discovering cures for it. The most recent among these cures is fasting, appropriately renamed "total food abstinence"! From an article self-assuredly titled "Fasting: An Old Cure for Fat, A New Treatment for Schizophrenia," we learn that:

Despite its dangers, a few physicians have begun to use fasting as a treatment for schizophrenia. The chronic mental disorder—with a constellation of possible mental symptoms from hallucinations to apathy to paranoia—afflicts more than two million Americans and costs the country more than $14 billion a year.[62]

Having so "identified" the alleged disease, the reader is presumably put in the properly receptive frame of mind to appreciate the selfless struggles of wise men in white coats who are trying to save the sanity of "more than two million Americans," not to mention the $14 billion. The author of this article, Steve Berman, has no doubts that schizophrenia is a disease. After all, we have already had one "breakthrough" in treating it. Now all we need is another one:

> But there have been no major breakthroughs in the battle against the disease since a French navy surgeon introduced phenothiazines in 1951. No one yet knows whether fasting will prove to be a comparable breakthrough. A limited number of tests augur well.[63]

Were the human misery exploited by these modern snake-oil merchants not so tragic, the scene now unfolding before us with respect to the "treatment of schizophrenia" would be hilarious. Psychiatrists don't know what schizophrenia is, and don't know how to diagnose it. At the same time, one group of psychiatrists claims to be able to cure it by feeding the "patients" huge doses of vitamins, while another group recommends withholding all food from them. It is hard to see how both claims could be true, although it is easy to see how both could be false.

Among those advocating starving schizophrenics are, not surprisingly, Russian psychiatrists, now widely recognized as the foremost diagnosticians of this dread disease:

> Other experiments with total food abstinence [*sic*] have been carried on at the prestigious Psychiatric Institute in

> Moscow. There, Professor Uri Nikolayev was the first to try fasting as a potential cure for schizophrenia. . . . He has seen a 65 percent improvement rate among his more than 7000 patients.[64]

Zionists called "schizophrenics"; starvation called "total food abstinence"; we had better laugh lest we weep.

Undeterred by all the marvelous "medical" treatments for schizophrenia, those who believe that schizophrenia is a "psychological disorder" continue to offer their "psychodynamic" treatments for it. In a review article, Arieti lists the contributions of eleven prominent psychotherapists to the treatment of schizophrenia. He then summarizes his own "technique" as aiming

> at reestablishing the bond of human relatedness with the patient, attacking psychotic symptoms with specific techniques, understanding the psychodynamic history, especially in the misinterpreted relations with the family, and helping the patient to unfold toward new, nonpsychotic patterns of living. Thus, although the psychotherapy of schizophrenia retains the interpretative technique and the uncovering of the repressed, as in the original psychoanalytic therapy, it expands in many directions. It is just as nourishing as it is interpretative. . . . Although at first the therapist assumes a parental role, he gradually becomes a peer of the patient.[65]

Although this passage faithfully reflects the fundamental decency of its author, it can hardly be said to contain any real information about what therapist and patient may and may not do to and with each other in the therapeutic situation or outside of it. Actually, what one of the therapists to whose pioneering work Arieti refers does with at least some of his schizophrenic patients we learn from the court records of a malpractice suit brought against him. In the late 1940s and early 1950s John Rosen proclaimed himself the possessor of a new and miraculous psychotherapeutic cure for schizophrenia, which he called "direct analysis." As we shall see, one ingredient of direct analysis is direct assault—the therapist beating the patient and calling it "treatment."

The patient, Alice Hammer, was an adult but legally incompetent person, placed under Rosen's care by her parents. The following are excerpts from the records of the trial court in the malpractice suit brought against Rosen by Alice Hammer's parents:

It was brought to the attention of the parent's family that the defendant made claims to dramatic success in the treatment of schizophrenic patients. The defendant was sought out, requested to, and did agree to treat the patient. Nurse H. Louise Wong, who attended the patient for 12 days during September 1948, testified that on two occasions she took the patient to the defendant for treatment. . . . After completion of the treatment on the first occasion, Nurse Wong observed that the patient's body was covered with bruises, and her clothes were torn and disheveled. . . . Apart from the testimony of Nurse Wong, there was ample evidence in the record of defendant's assaults of the patient on various occasions in the course of his treatments. Mrs. Hammer testified that after treatments she observed her daughter was "beaten up" and had "blue eyes"; that her daughter returned from treatments "black and blue." Mrs. Hammer also testified to conversations with the defendant wherein he stated that the assaults complained of were part of the treatment.[66]

In his defense, Dr. Rosen argued,

that the treatment was knowingly and freely consented to by reason of the fact that the patient's mother testified that if beating was a means of cure, she was agreeable to the treatment.[67]

The appeals court was not impressed.[68] Beating mental patients was, of course, not invented by John Rosen, his innovation having been limited to doing it in the relative openness of his private office rather than behind the locked doors of a mental hospital.

We do not hear much any more about direct analysis. It has been replaced by other revolutionary treatments for schizophrenia, such as the following, recently announced in the pages of the *Schizophrenia Bulletin,* a publication of the National Institute of Mental Health. In conjunction with megavitamins and beatings, it shows us as clearly as anything could that schizophrenia is not a psychiatric syndrome but a scientific scandal. The author, Antonio Parras, assistant professor of psychiatry at New York Medical College, explains that:

The purpose of the Lounge is to provide an environment that is relatively unthreatening and promotes growth. . . . The Lounge Program got under way at Maimonides Community Mental Health Center in October 1971. Patients were informed that they could come on Tuesday afternoons to get their prescriptions renewed. It was also mentioned that the Lounge was an informal setting where they could, if they wished, meet with other patients and staff. Patients were told to feel free to use the facilities of the Lounge Hall, which included pool, card games, arts and crafts, music, and refreshments. . . . This preliminary report indicates that the Lounge can be beneficial to chronic schizophrenics. . . . This treatment philosophy can be applied to a chronic inpatient ward. . . . It can be an immense source material for studies in schizophrenia.[69]

It is more likely that programs and reports such as this will be "an immense source material" for studies in the scientific scandals which modern psychiatrists have been able to pull off—publishing their fables and fakeries in prestigious medical and scientific journals, confusing a lounge with a Lounge, and promoting this literalized medical metaphor, under the imprimatur of the National Institute of Mental Health, as a "treatment" for "schizophrenia." [70]

Small wonder that everyone is now convinced that schizophrenia is a disease. Paresis is a disease for one reason only: because the paretic patient suffers from a demonstrable abnormality of his brain. Schizophrenia is a disease for many reasons: because the schizophrenic patient suffers from an abnormality of his brain which medical science is on the verge of demonstrating; because he suffers and makes others suffer; because he is confined in a mental hospital; because he receives psychiatric treatment; and because his disease is expensive. This last criterion—the latest, and perhaps the most characteristically American, addition to the criteria of schizophrenia—is undoubtedly the most imaginative and the most humorous.

The typical form of this method for claiming that schizophrenia is an illness—or, better, for implying that it is so obviously an illness as to make any further discussion of the question seem imbecilic—is to document the carefully calculated cost of the "disease" and its "treatment." Such an effort is exemplified by a paper written by John Gunderson and Loren Mosher. Mosher is, appropriately, the chief of the Center for Studies of Schizophrenia at the National Institute of Mental Health. As a modern "dynamic" psychiatrist and a devotee of Laing, Mosher is clearly unfamiliar with medicine. But as a federal bureaucrat, he is familiar indeed with money. Thus, he and Gunderson write:

The cost of schizophrenia has been estimated at $11.6 to $19.5 billion annually. About two-thirds of this cost is due to lack of productivity by schizophrenic patients and about one-fifth to treatment costs. The estimates might be considerably higher if better figures were available on the cost of maintaining patients in the community.[71]

This is pure rhetoric. By discussing the "lack of productivity" and "treatment" of "schizophrenics" as if they were discussing the lack of productivity and treatment of patients with strokes, Gunderson and Mosher make it seem as if schizophrenia were, in fact, a disease. Actually, many people are "unproductive"—in the sense that they produce less than others in comparable circumstances, or less than they might if they exerted themselves more, or because they are lazy or are supported by others—for reasons that have nothing to do with illness and health. For example, children and college students, the rich and the retired, are all "unproductive." To none of them, however, do psychiatrists writing about the cost of schizophrenia compare schizophrenics. In this way psychiatrists manage to compose an inflated balance sheet of staggering costs attributable solely to "schizophrenia." The following excerpt illustrates such a rhetorical effect and, presumably, a corresponding political aim:

In 1968 the estimated cost of all mental illness was placed at $21 billion, of which $17 billion was attributed to loss of productivity. . . . Schizophrenic patients undoubtedly contribute a disproportionately large proportion of this estimate. . . . It seems safe to estimate that schizophrenics living in the community account for 50 percent of the loss of productivity each year, or about $7.5 billion in 1968.[72]

The authors then remark on unemployed schizophrenics, implying that some persons are unemployed because they cannot get jobs, and others because they are afflicted with the disease called "schizophrenia." By implying this distinction rather than explicating it, they conceal the assumption that schizophrenia is a disease, thus rendering it unavailable for scrutiny. "Taking a prevalence rate of 2 to 3 percent for schizophrenia," they write, "the 75 percent of all schizophrenics who are unemployed contribute 3 to 4 million to the total number of unemployed." [73]

Ironically, Gunderson and Mosher acknowledge that although in the past the field for studying and influencing paresis might have been the neuropathology laboratory and the chemotherapy research institute, it is now the Congress and the United States Mint. To make this point—though it is not the point *they* say they are making—the authors cite, with unbounded approval, Mosher's boss, Bertram S. Brown, the director of the National Institute of Mental Health. According to Brown, "The future of mental health and mental retardation is in the area of economics, taxation, and finance." [74] If this is so, why are psychiatric residents taught Bleuler and Freud instead of Marx and von Mises? Because what Gunderson and Mosher mean is not that psychiatrists should know more about economics, but that they should become more adept at robbing the national treasury:

> We need to demonstrate that it costs more not to treat someone than it does to provide care. If doubling the cost of treatment makes it possible to halve the loss of productivity, about $2 billion a year will be saved. [75]

Here, then, we are face to face with the inexorable consequences of psychiatry as a state-supported priesthood and of its collectivistic-positivistic perspective of treating persons as defective objects. The traditional reasons and justifications for treatment in medicine have been, first, that the patient has a disease; second, that he wants and consents to treatment for it;

and third, that a physician agrees to treat him. Gunderson and Mosher now add a fourth justification for treatment to this list—one, moreover, that has long been the favorite therapeutic justification among Marxists, Communists, and National Socialists: namely, that treating the patient is in the best economic interests of society. It is important to articulate the corollary of this rule: that treatment should be unavailable, or perhaps even prohibited, if it is not in the best economic interests of society. The patients' desire and consent for treatment, and the physician's freedom to treat or eschew treatment, are, of course, all matters potentially—and, in the so-called mental health field, actually—at odds with the economic-therapeutic principle enunciated by Gunderson and Mosher. This is hardly surprising. The principle they propose is for the benefit of the bureaucrats whose views Brown and Mosher represent, that is, the state-employed psychiatrist-policemen. After all, it is they, not the patients, who are the recipients of the funds here debated.

Some of this has, of course, always been true, but a new twist has been added to it in modern collectivistic-coercive psychiatry. What has always been true is that patients got the treatment and doctors got the money. But traditionally, the patients wanted the treatment, and they paid the doctors. In the new arrangement "patients" get "treatments" they do not want, and the state pays the psychiatrists for coercing, confining, and chemically mutilating its recalcitrant citizens.

At the beginning of this chapter I emphasized that the primary phenomenon in hospital psychiatry is, and has always been, social deviance, or being a nuisance to others, and its control or repression by means of psychiatric incarceration; and that the notion of schizophrenia was superimposed on it and cannot be dealt with in isolation from it.

Although I have made some references to Soviet psychiatry, most of what I have said so far has been about psychiatry in the so-called free societies. Let us now apply these observations and reflections to psychiatry in so-called totalitarian societies. In such societies the relationship between psychiatrist and mental patient is so paternalistic and coercive that I consider it misleading even to refer to them as "doctor" and "patient." In the Soviet Union patients, especially mental patients, are more like prisoners on parole than free citizens contracting for medical services, and physicians, especially psychiatrists, are more like parole officers than physicians providing medical services. The result is that personal and social problems of all kinds, and especially political deviance, are defined and treated as psychiatric diseases even more readily in the USSR than in the US or the UK.

J. K. Wing, a British psychiatrist who had visited the Soviet Union on four occasions, accounts for some of the differences between Russian and British psychiatry in this way:

> The diagnostic system used by many Soviet psychiatrists is different from that incorporated in the International Classification of Diseases. In particular, the term "schizophrenia" is used to describe conditions which British psychiatrists would label in other ways. This clinical difference partly explains the different concept of "criminal responsibility," but another large component of the difference is political rather than medical.[76]

No physician anywhere would acknowledge that there are political reasons for diagnosing lobar pneumonia or myocardial infarction differently in capitalist and communist countries. Although American and British psychiatrists are now beginning to acknowledge that there are political reasons for diagnosing schizophrenia differently in their countries and in Russia, they continue to insist that schizophrenia is, nevertheless, a disease, just like lobar pneumonia and myocardial infarction. Because some Russian psychiatrists "misuse" the names of certain psychiatric diseases, so these Western psychiatrists argue, is no reason for doubting the validity of the diagnosis when "correctly" applied, or the "reality" of the disease it names. Wing actually describes the way the term *schizophrenia* is used in Russia to justify controlling deviants, but this seems not to affect his acceptance of the label as the name of a bona fide medical disease:

> As we have already seen, the concept of mental illness, particularly schizophrenia, is a good deal wider [in the USSR] than in the UK, including quite a lot of what we would call personality disorder. None of the people whose case histories I have heard were suffering from schizophrenia in the same sense of the florid central syndrome recognized by psychiatrists everywhere. There are two main groups: one composed of people who had been admitted [*sic*] to mental hospitals long before they had become political dissenters (though not for what I would call "schizophrenia"); the other comprising people who have developed complex economic and social theories which they put forward as alternatives to currently orthodox Marxism. . . . Most British psychiatrists would probably not make a diagnosis of schizophrenia (or any kind of mental illness) in such cases.[77]

Obviously, the distinction between voluntary and involuntary mental hospitalization is quite meaningless in Russia. All mental patients are actually like prisoners or paroled prisoners: none is, or feels, free to decide whether he should be treated in the hospital, clinic, or not at all. Although Wing seems rather insensitive about the issue of human rights in psychiatry, he notes that while on paper there is a difference between committed and voluntary mental patients, it is a difference not demonstrable in practice:

I tried to discover whether a patient not under certificate is free to leave the hospital "against advice," but it seemed very difficult for my informants to envisage such a case. After a great deal of questioning they did finally say that it would be possible but they could not recall it happening.[78]

It does not seem to occur to Wing that in a country where people cannot even move from one city to another without the permission of the authorities, it would not occur to them to try to leave mental hospitals "against advice." * And it does not seem to occur to psychiatrists—or to the biologists, chemists, and geneticists who base their work on psychiatric diagnoses—that "schizophrenia" has more to do with freedom and slavery

---

* It is, of course, as meaningless and misleading to try to distinguish between voluntary and involuntary mental hospitalization in Russia as it is to try to distinguish between amateur and professional athletics in that country. As we know, however, in the Olympic Games, the free or non-Communist nations of the world accept Russian athletes as if they were amateurs. Similarly, in international medical meetings and organizations, free or non-Communist physicians accept Russian psychiatrists as regular physicians, and Russian mental patients as regular patients. Moreover, since even in the non-Communist world medicine is, as it were, a house divided against itself—comprising both free and unfree patients and physicians—the same self-destructive pattern of behavior is displayed by "real" doctors in free societies toward "fake" doctors or psychiatrists and their patients: that is, physicians accept psychiatrists as if they were regular physicians, and mental patients as if they were regular patients. Through these acts of capitulation and compliance, amateur athletes and individualistic physicians, and all those who support the values their roles embody, in effect commit suicide: [79] by accepting Russian athletes as amateurs, Western athletes participate in liquidating a distinction important in their society but not in Communist society; likewise, by accepting physicians who are agents of the state as if they were agents of the individual, individualistic physicians participate in liquidating a distinction essential for their work but not for that of their collectivistic colleagues. This process, unless it is reversed, can lead only to the gradual erosion and ultimate disappearance of the values and identities of the amateur sportsman in athletics and the physician as the agent of his patient in medicine.

than with health and disease, more with semiology than with biology, more, in short, with politics than with genetics.

To place my foregoing remarks about schizophrenia in proper perspective, it is now necessary, first, to raise and confront some basic ethical and political questions; and second, to review briefly our traditional ideas about illness, our traditional methods for identifying it, and the metamorphoses of these ideas and methods in modern psychiatry.

I submit that there are some basic ethical and political questions that are anterior—morally, logically, and empirically —to the sorts of questions into which psychiatrists are fond of plunging without the observance of any of the preliminary decencies they ought to observe. The questions are these: Should psychiatrists (or other physicians) have the right to diagnose a person as schizophrenic if that person, the alleged "patient," does not seek psychiatric help? Should they have the right to do so if the "patient" explicitly objects to being diagnosed?

I think these questions are interesting because, despite their seeming simplicity, they have apparently never been asked in psychiatry. The whole history of psychiatry seems to be based on the premise—inexplicit but all the more important—that psychiatrists have the right to "diagnose" anyone, anywhere, living or dead, whether he or she likes it or not. I consider this premise at once ridiculous and repellent. I believe we must repudiate it as rapidly and as radically as we can—as much for our own sake as healers, physicians, and scientists, as for the sake of our involuntary clients as victims, patients, and human beings.

I point here to a very simple, but very important, matter that touches the heart, if not the mind, of everyone who has ever been a sufferer or a healer; in short, of everyone. That matter is the degree to which our minds are inviolably our own.

In all societies—free and unfree—there is a sphere of individual privacy which the authorities, the state, do not violate (except under exceptional circumstances). Thus, certain intimate personal possessions, such as socks and pipes, books and snapshots, are generally recognized as a person's very own, which means that he can sort them and name them as he wishes. But there are other things, less tangible but no less real, which people also regard as intimate personal possessions, such as their dreams, their opinions, their names. Actually, the privacy of these treasured nonmaterial possessions is now generally less well protected than the privacy of such trivial material possessions as I have mentioned. It is a remarkable paradox, and remarkably unappreciated, that a psychiatrist cannot go uninvited into a man's home and rename his dog, but he can go into his home uninvited and rename him. This is one of the ways in which John Doe becomes a "schizophrenic patient."

We must, therefore, ask ourselves some hard questions. What is more precious to us: the privacy of our relations to our pets or to our parents? What requires, and deserves, greater protection from authorities (regardless of who they are or what their motives may be): our right to the privacy of our home or to the privacy of our mind? Our right to name our dog or to name ourselves? It is questions such as these that lie behind the semantic curtain of psychiatric nosology, and it is this curtain which conceals—from laymen and professionals alike—the epistemological blunders and existential brutalities of psychiatry.

There is, moreover, a compelling similarity between the premise that psychiatrists out to have a right to "diagnose" people without their consent or even against their will, and the premise that psychiatrists ought to have a right to "treat" people without their consent and even against their will. I neither wish to, nor could, repeat here the objections I have advanced against this latter practice.[80] Let me say only that insofar as psychiatrists are granted the privilege in free societies to treat adult persons against their will—a privilege which other physicians and professional persons do not enjoy—psychiatry becomes assimilated to jurisprudence and penology; in short, it becomes a discipline for controlling deviance, not for curing diseases. Since this is in fact the case now, worldwide, it seems to me absurd, to put it mildly, to consider the deviant acts which psychiatrists now control—and which of course differ from culture to culture and class to class—as diseases. Furthermore, insofar as in totalitarian societies not only psychiatrists but all physicians are granted the privilege—indeed, have the duty imposed on them—to "treat" persons against their will, there is a difference between the moral and political underpinnings of the medical and psychiatric professions in "free" and totalitarian societies which alters significantly not only their empirical observations, but the very languages in which they are framed.

We are now ready to turn to the remaining unarticulated epistemological problem underlying the problem of schizophrenia—namely, the nature of our traditional medical ideas about what constitutes illness and our traditional methods for identifying it; the expansion and transformation of these ideas and methods in modern psychiatry; and the consequences of these changes as manifested by the fact that when people now call something an illness, or someone sick (and especially mentally sick), they do not necessarily mean anything like what the term originally meant, although they might believe or claim that they do.

Toward the middle of the last century, as we saw, disease was defined as histopathology or pathophysiology. Injuries, infections, metabolic disorders, and tumors were thus the characteristic classes of diseases. The accepted scientific method for demonstrating such diseases consisted, first, of identifying their morphological characteristics by postmortem examination of organs and tissues; and second, of ascertaining, by means of systematic observations and experiments, preferably on animals, their origins or causes. Paresis meets this criterion of disease. Schizophrenia does not—at least, until now, it has not.

However, since this conclusion has, in the main, been unacceptable to physicians and laymen alike, there has been a concerted effort ever since Bleuler announced his "discovery" of schizophrenia—and, indeed, even prior to it!—to change the criteria of what constitutes disease and the corresponding ground rules for demonstrating it. In the course of this process several new criteria of disease, and corresponding methods for demonstrating its presence, have been generated. I have touched on all of them, and it will suffice now to summarize this important metamorphosis in medical epistemology.

The classic Virchowian model of disease was first expanded to include psychopathology. This was accomplished by Kraepelin, Bleuler, Freud, and their followers. Simultaneously, or close on its heels, there arose the practice of inferring disease from medical or psychiatric contact, or the patient role. If a person visited a physician and complained to him, then he had "symptoms" which ipso facto pointed to the presence of a disease. And if the person was confined in a mental hospital, then he was ipso facto suffering from a mental disease. The former inference justified treating "patients" without demonstrable diseases; the latter justified incarcerating them.

With the development of more effective therapeutic methods in the 1920s and 1930s, and especially since the 1940s, it became acceptable to infer disease from the patient's alleged response to treatment. A person might thus have been given antibiotics or hormones, and if they made him feel better, then his pretreatment "condition" was regarded as an illness. This criterion and method were ideally suited to psychiatry, especially institutional psychiatry, authenticating such interventions as insulin shock, electroshock, lobotomy, and psychophar-macologicals as treatments, and schizophrenia and countless other "conditions" as diseases.

Finally, with the steady collectivization of medical practice and the spreading of its costs to third parties, especially the state, since the 1950s, there arose the economic criterion and method of measuring diseases—namely, its cost in terms of unemployment, underemployment, and funds expended for medical care. By this criterion schizophrenia qualifies as the "number one health problem" in the nation, and indeed in the world.

In concluding this chapter I want to articulate, more explicitly than I have heretofore, which justifications of treatment—especially in psychiatry—I object to and why, and which I support and why. I might be able to do this best, and most concisely, by reference to a recent psychiatric statement on the treatment of schizophrenia which exemplifies many of the epistemological errors to which I have pointed already.

Hans Huessy, an American psychiatrist, asserts that:

An understanding of causes is important for prevention, but not for treatment. . . . We can treat the acute symptoms of schizophrenia by medical means despite our lack of knowledge as to this disorder's causes. Therapies that are justified on the basis of causes should always be suspect, since the only valid justification for therapeutic intervention is that it produces improvement.[81]

This statement—which condenses an incredible amount of stupidity, immorality, and just plain wrongheadedness into a mere three sentences—appeared in a prestigious psychiatric journal and faithfully reflects a perspective on therapy that is, if not universal, at least prevalent. Its author belittles the importance of causes, or etiology, in therapy. Such a position is simply erroneous. Whether a persons' failing vision is caused by syphilitic optic atrophy or a tumor pressing on his optic chiasma is essential for selecting and suggesting the proper treatment for him.

This author also asserts that he can treat "the acute symptoms of schizophrenia" by medical means, meaning drugs, without knowing the cause of schizophrenia. However, he has not established either that schizophrenia is a disease or that the alleged patient wants to be treated; and he has implied, misleadingly, that because the behavior of people called "schizophrenic" can be changed by drugs, schizophrenia is a disease. That this argument, popular in psychiatry today, is false is easily demonstrated by asserting a parallel argument: because the behavior of ordinary or so-called normal people can be changed by giving them alcohol, which is a drug, normality is a disease and drinking alcohol is a treatment.

Huessy's greatest intellectual obtuseness and moral depravity lie, however, in his assertion that "the only valid justification for therapeutic intervention is that it produces improvement." This is a frankly ethical statement: it is an assertion about a particular value ("improvement") justifying a particular kind of act ("therapeutic intervention").

Actually, there are at least three distinct categories of facts that may be used to justify therapy.[82] First is the fact that the patient has a disease; in this view, what justifies mastectomy, for example, is that the patient has breast cancer. Second is the fact that the therapy is effective; in this view, what justifies mastectomy is that it cures the cancer. Both of these considerations are relevant to assessing therapeutic interventions: the first legitimizes therapy on the grounds of the patient's illness, the second on the grounds of the effectiveness of the physician's interventions.

What is missing? The morally and politically most relevant—in fact, from this point of view, the only really relevant—consideration: namely, consent. In this—ethical, legal, and political—view, what justifies mastectomy is the fact that the patient gives informed consent to the operation and the surgeon is willing to perform it. The role of consent, especially for the history and epistemology of psychiatry, is so overarching in importance that it is impossible to exaggerate it. One might even argue—and though such an argument is incomplete, it is nevertheless important—that it is consent and consent alone that justifies cure and treatment (as opposed to control and torture).

Although it is a useful guidepost to clear thinking and speaking to insist that there can be no treatment without illness, it is obvious that there can be medical and surgical intervention without illness: for example, abortion or vasectomy. (To be sure, in American law, unwanted pregnancy is now a disease, but this is a linguistic and legal aberration that does not justify further comment here.) Similarly, physicians and surgeons have employed methods in the past, and continue to employ methods today, that were and are therapeutically worthless, or even harmful. Was venesection (bloodletting) a therapy? Is electroshock (mindletting) a therapy? Clearly, unless we are prepared to rewrite medical history, eliminating what is worthless as we go along, we cannot define therapy by its effectiveness.

What remains, then, is consent to therapy. Virtually all modern medical therapy in free societies, administered to conscious adults, conforms to the requirement of consent. The sole exception is psychiatric therapy. I have emphasized this ethical and political dimension of illness and treatment because by viewing psychiatric illnesses and treatments through the moral magnifying instrument which it provides, we glimpse a new image and definition of schizophrenia (and some of the other so-called major functional psychoses). By looking through this metaphorical microscope, we can distinguish among various diseases and treatments, not according to morphological (that is, anatomical or histological) criteria, but according to moral (and legal, political, and so on) criteria.

We may thus identify one class of diseases—such as cancer of the breast or hypertension—which physicians never treat (and, in free societies, are forbidden to treat) without the explicit consent of the patient.

We may identify another class—such as strokes or injuries causing unconsciousness—which physicians treat without the explicit consent of the patient because he cannot give consent, permission in such cases being given by relatives or other legally recognized authorities.

We may identify a third class—such as tuberculosis or hepatitis—in which cases, although certain social restrictions may be placed on the patients because of their illness, physicians in free societies are still debarred by law from treatment without the patient's consent.

Finally, we may identify a fourth class of "diseases"—such as schizophrenia or manic-depressive psychosis—which physicians are permitted to treat in the face of explicit objection against treatment by the alleged patient. It is precisely the social reality of this sort of "treatment," and the corresponding need to confine by force persons objecting to it, that, as I indicated earlier, generates the image (*mirage* might be a better word for it) of certain psychiatric diseases or syndromes, particularly schizophrenia.[83] In this view schizophrenia could be said to be that disease which justifies the imposition of psychiatric treatment on the patient—regardless of whether he consents to it or not, and, of course, regardless of whether it helps or harms him.*

Madness, as I suggested some time ago, is, in a sense, manufactured by mad-doctors.[84] In other words, psychiatry creates

* This latter judgment is rendered moot by psychiatric confinement: individuals who do not want certain interventions imposed on them are likely to regard them as ipso facto harmful or noxious; whereas psychiatrists and other socially authenticated authorities responsible for imposing such interventions on unwilling "patients" are likely to regard them as helpful or therapeutic if they make the "patients" more docile, socially conforming, and receptive to further "treatment."

schizophrenia, or, more precisely, psychiatrists create schizophrenics. It is important that we be very clear in just what sense they do so, and what the practical implications of this view are for our attitude toward the so-called problem of schizophrenia.

The sense in which I mean that psychiatry creates schizophrenia is readily illustrated by the analogy between institutional psychiatry and involuntary servitude. If there is no slavery, there can be no slaves. In other words, the identity of an individual as a slave depends on the existence of the social system of slavery. Hence, if slavery is abolished, slaves disappear. This does not mean that certain kinds of persons who might previously have been slaves, or who might like to be slaves, also disappear; there assuredly remain persons who are black, or helpless, or uneducated, or stupid, or submissive, or lazy. But if there is no slavery, none of them can be a slave.

Similarly, if there is no psychiatry, there can be no schizophrenics. In other words, the identity of an individual as a schizophrenic depends on the existence of the social system of (institutional) psychiatry. Hence, if psychiatry is abolished, schizophrenics disappear. This does not mean that certain kinds of persons who might previously have been schizophrenics, or who might like to be schizophrenics, also disappear; there assuredly remain persons who are incompetent, or self-absorbed, or who reject their "real" roles, or who offend others in some other ways. But if there is no psychiatry, none of them can be schizophrenic.

To be sure, the abolition of slavery only frees the slave. It does not make him educated, self-sufficient, attractive, employable, or physically healthy; it only sets him free from his master. Similarly, the abolition of psychiatry would only free the schizophrenic. It would not make him competent, self-sufficient, attractive, employable, or "mentally healthy." It would only set him free from his psychiatrist.

It would, of course, be absurd to seek the advancement of the slave within the slave system, and in particular from his master. It is similarly absurd to seek the "treatment" of the schizophrenic within the psychiatric system, and in particular from his psychiatrist. The "improvement" of slaves and schizophrenics is a clearly desirable goal. But, like all goals, if it is not pursued intelligently and properly, it might as well not be pursued at all.

Chapter 4

Psychiatry and Matrimony: Arrangements for Living

THERE ARE MANY REASONS why the medical perspective on schizophrenia has proved so popular and persistent: it is historically well grounded in the origin, structure, and function of the modern mental hospital; it is psychologically legitimized in the language of psychiatry; it is consistent with the contemporary predilection for viewing the tragedies of life through the disease-colored glasses of medicine; and it provides socially acceptable methods for coping with certain economic, moral, political, and personal problems which would otherwise have to be dealt with in untried and unfamiliar ways. Moreover, there may be still another reason for the popularity and persistence of the so-called medical model of schizophrenia: no other model of comparable scope and power has been offered for it.[1] Nor, indeed, could such a superior model possibly be offered. The greatest symbolic and social power of "schizophrenia" lies precisely in its being inextricably tied to the idea of disease and the institution of medicine. Thus, an effort to offer a nonmedical model for schizophrenia is about as feasible, and futile, as would be the effort to offer a nontheological model for the Eucharist.

It has long seemed to me that the only way to cope with the seemingly insoluble problems of psychiatry is by completely rejecting the traditional quasi-medical perspective on them and by viewing them instead as arising not simply out of the so-called patient's head or brain or mind but rather out of a rich network of relations in which patient and psychiatrist are merely the two most prominent protagonists.

The idea that schizophrenia is not simply a problem of something going wrong in the brain or mind of the so-called patient; that it is, still in the language of contemporary psychiatry, not just an intrapersonal, but also an interpersonal, problem; or, to put it more plainly and precisely, that it is not only a problem posed, but also a solution proposed, in a complex network of relationships comprising the patient, his or her family, the psychiatrist, the mental hospital system, and society as a whole—this existential, dramaturgic, and psychosocial perspective on schizophrenia is actually no longer brand new.[2] It has, however, not helped to clarify the problem of schizophrenia as much as had been expected, mainly, I think, because it has given rise to new "etiological theories" of this "disease," still resting on and replicating the classical disease model of syphilis. Instead of the Treponema pallidum "driving the patient crazy," it is the "schizophrenogenic" mother, father, family, religion, economic system, or society as a whole that is now, in these new psychiatric and anti-psychiatric theories, "driving the patient crazy." The image thus projected onto our mental screens, though perhaps more accurate than that projected by the paradigm of paresis it seeks to displace, is still completely out of focus; it cannot account for the facts of psychiatric life and does not give us an intellectually and morally satisfying lever in trying to deal with them.

If we take the truly human, totally nonmedical, perspective on so-called schizophrenia seriously, it follows that what we need is not a model of the "patient" at all—whether of his brain, mind, or behavior. Instead, what we need is a model of the whole social situation or drama of which the relationship between the "schizophrenic patient" and his "significant others" is a part, and in which "schizophrenia" is somehow generated. We do not have far to look for such a model. I shall try to show that marriage—especially of the traditional, arranged sort—

supplies us with a powerful paradigm for interpreting the psychiatrist-patient relationship. In this scheme we shall view the psychiatrist as the husband, the psychotic as the wife, and schizophrenia as the diagnosis/child and/or schizophrenic-incompetency/feminine-inferiority which the patient/wife acquires before the commitment/wedding or receives from the psychiatrist/husband after it; we shall keep in mind that, above all, it is the psychiatric-matrimonial relationship that defines and legitimizes the condition and status of each partner—as psychiatrist/husband and as patient/wife.

Let us review briefly the principal features of the institution of matrimony in its traditional form of arranged marriage, which will be our model for clarifying arranged or institutional psychiatry.

Marriage is a universal social arrangement whose precise patterns vary considerably from place to place and from time to time. As an institution, matrimony performs countless personal and social functions, from the satisfaction of sexual needs to the regulation of social relations and the replenishment of the race.[3] For our present purposes it will suffice to note that the marriage relationship, like the psychiatric relationship, has three distinct phases: the initiation of the relationship; the "chronic" state of the relationship; and the termination of the relationship. For arranged marriages, the initiation and termination phases are remarkably similar among quite diverse cultures. This is consistent with the fact that the initiation of the relationship—insofar as it is "arranged" *for,* rather than *by,* the prospective husband and wife—usually forms an integral part of a patriarchal kinship system. In such a system marriage is a transaction not so much between the two (ostensible) partners, but rather between their respective chiefs, clans, or families. Moreover, in pre-Christian marriage, termination, like initiation, was also frequently a bargain between the chiefs of the clans concerned: "As far as the [Jewish] 'law' stood at the time of Jesus, a marriage could at any time be terminated arbitrarily by the husband, while no corresponding power whatsoever existed for the wife." [4]

The subsequent course of Western marriage was shaped primarily by the religion of Christianity, and secondarily by the economics of feudalism. Marriage became one of the holy sacraments in the fourth century, and was declared to be indissoluble around the ninth century. It was thus a holy or sacred institution for a millennium and a half when, after the French Revolution, it was quickly secularized. During the nineteenth century civil marriage became compulsory by law throughout most of Europe. At present, only in Greece, Israel (for Jews only), and the Vatican City is a religious marriage ceremony compulsory.[5]

Although among the better-educated classes of Europe, America, Russia, and, increasingly, Japan, the romantic model of marriage, with the partners doing the choosing, now predominates, the majority of marriages throughout the world are still arranged, with the partners being assigned to each other. In Africa, in southeastern Europe, and in the Near East and the Orient, arranged marriages continue to be the rule. The go-betweens or marriage brokers are usually older and respected persons who may or may not be relatives, and who may or may not be paid for their services. In such marriages, writes Judson Taylor Landis, "From the first inquiries of the go-between to the final arrangements, economic considerations are in the forefront." [6]

Wherever arranged marriage was institutionalized, it was thus closely tied to the patriarchal family as a political-religious system of social control, and to its characteristic economic patterns for regulating the acquisition, distribution, and inheritance of goods and services. Hence, where the support for these arrangements is undermined or removed, as they are in industrial societies in the West and in Communist societies in the East, arranged marriages are quickly replaced by marriages in which the partners do the choosing. "Communism," writes Landis, "theoretically eliminates the economic basis of marriage and matchmaking; . . . countries that have adopted communism have wiped out the foundations of arranged marriages and have substituted the free choice of individual marriage partners." [7] Where the choice to marry is legitimized as an individual decision, the choice to divorce with similar ease cannot lag too far behind.

Social organization, or the orderly arrangement of persons in groups, requires that individuals be assigned to clearly identified spaces, both physical and symbolic. One of the main functions of matrimony as a social institution is to locate persons, in the physical space known as the home, and in the symbolic spaces known as the roles of husband, wife, child, and so on. It is in this space- and role-assigning function that matrimony and institutional psychiatry resemble each other so crucially.

The view that matrimony is, in part at least, a matter of housing, though obvious enough, needs to be made fully explicit here. The idea is already articulated in the Old Testament, in connection with the specification of the grounds for divorce: "When a man hath taken a wife, and married her, and it comes to pass that she find no favor in his eyes, because he hath found some uncleanness in her; then let him write her a bill of divorcement, and give it in her hand, and send her out of his house." [8] The house here, let us note, is the husband's. Hence it is the woman, not the man, who is made homeless by divorce.

St. Matthew objects to this traditional Jewish law and proposes to reform it. Divorce, he asserts, is morally permissible only for fornication. Actually, what he has in mind is still a masculine sanction for a feminine transgression: "It hath been said, Whosoever shall put away his wife, let him give her a writing of divorcement: But I say unto you, That whosoever shall put away his wife, saving for the cause of fornication, causeth her to commit adultery." [9]

The Biblical English phrase to "put away" one's wife, meaning to divorce her, has, of course, become a euphemism for committing her to a madhouse. I shall make further comment on this presently.

The change in divorce laws from the Old to the New Testament reflects the tightening, and perhaps the clearer articulation, of one of the great sins—perhaps even the greatest—in the Judeo-Christian ethic: namely, personal autonomy, self-control over one's own body and mind, or, more specifically, over one's own sexual and mental acts. With respect to sexual acts, this new Christian ethic is clearly articulated, for example, in I Corinthians, where Paul explains that "It is good for a man not to touch a woman. Nevertheless, to avoid fornication, let every man have his own wife, and let every woman have her own husband." [10] Why is it, as he later puts it, better to "marry than to burn"? [11] Because in marriage husband and wife relinquish control over their bodies to their partners: "The wife hath not power of her own body, but her husband; and likewise also the husband hath not power of his own body, but the wife." [12]

This relinquishing of self-control over the body by husband and wife makes each of them resemble the truly continent person whose body belongs wholly to God: "But I speak this by permission [says Paul], and not of commandment. For I would that all men were even as I myself. . . . I say therefore to the unmarried and the widows, It is good for them if they abide even as I. But if they cannot contain, let them marry: for it is better to marry than to burn." [13]

It is here, too, that Paul issues his command—in opposition to traditional Jewish law and custom—against divorce. He does so, moreover, in a language that is (in English) striking in its allusiveness to the parallel between husbands disposing of their wives by divorce and by commitment: "And let not the husband put away his wife." [14]

Christian marriage is thus sacrament. The union between husband and wife is justified, indeed exalted, because it "parallels, imitates, and participates in, so far as possible, the closeness and love exchanged between Christ and his bride, the Church." [15] This is why, in the Christian ethic, "putting asunder" what God has united is a mortal sin, and why psychiatric confinement of one marital partner by the other, or "putting away," is a veritable medical blessing. When a Christian husband "puts away" his wife or, more rarely, vice versa, he or she does not violate the sacred vows of marriage; on the contrary, such a person is regarded as saving the soul or the "mental health" of his or her partner, and also as saving their union.

Actually, husbands and wives often find their association intolerable and seek some way of dissolving it, or at least allaying the pain caused by it, by putting distance between themselves. Divorce, if it is an economically, morally, and personally acceptable option, is the most obvious solution to this problem. If it is not acceptable, husbands and wives have two other basic options, one age-old, the other relatively recent: murder and mental hospitalization. Murder has the disadvantage of producing a corpse, but this handicap has been surmounted, especially in devoutly religious societies, by excusing the act as a product of the "heat of passion," an explanation considered especially appealing when the passion is that of a man defending his honor defiled by an unfaithful wife.* Mental hospitalization has the advantage of accomplishing the same result as mur-

* Clarence Darrow is supposed to have said that he was for divorce because he was against murder. In other words, it is better that husband and wife divorce rather than commit violence against each other. And it is better that psychiatrist and "psychotic" divorce—both being free, when they have had enough of each other, to leave their partners—rather than commit violence against each other, the psychiatrist by incarcerating the patient, and the patient by assaulting the psychiatrist.

der, but without leaving a corpse; the handling of the product so created, aptly called the "living dead," is moreover readily justified by appeals to its characteristic property, namely, madness.

Until recently, women could not live alone. Even today they cannot do so except in societies that are highly developed both culturally and economically, and then only in the face of the greatest handicaps. Accordingly, women had to, and still have to, make their homes under the protection of, or at least with, others, mainly men.

In the past, a woman had three basic choices of domicile: living with her father (or his surrogate, such as uncle, brother, or brother-in-law), her husband, or God. In each of these arrangements the woman's identity was defined by her relationship and subordination to a man or male figure—father, husband, and Jesus—and each defined a particular female role —old maid, wife, and nun (or "bride of Jesus").

The creation of madhouses and insane asylums, and then of hospital psychiatry as an accredited social institution, in part replaced one of these arrangements, and in part added a new arrangement to them. A woman could now choose to be not only an old maid, wife, or nun—but also a madwoman. This option to choose, or be chosen for, a career of madness simultaneously replaced and supplemented the option to choose, or be chosen for, a career of religiosity. Hence the intimate association, in modern psychiatric thought and in modern "intellectually sophisticated" thought generally, between so-called excessive religiosity and madness—madness supposedly often being manifested by "excessive religiosity," and "excessive religiosity" often being regarded as a cause of madness.

Moreover, although a man could, in principle at least, establish a home for himself independently of a father, wife, or

Church, he, too, was under immense social pressure to opt for one of these home-making arrangements. And after the facilities of institutional psychiatry were added to the available home-making arrangements, men also could, and were indeed compelled to, take advantage of the opportunities it offered. Hence, the madhouse and mental hospital became a "home" for both men and women—more so for one sex or the other, depending on whatever factors (which vary from place to place and from time to time) make members of one or the other group more helpless and homeless, and thus in need of the facilities provided by such "orphanages" for adults.

Once we see chronic, and especially hospitalized, mental patienthood in general, and schizophrenia in particular, as a career or role, its connection with marriage, especially for women, becomes apparent. In all (patriarchal) societies women face a choice between two basic careers—matrimony and becoming a wife, or eschewing matrimony and becoming something else. But what—especially until recent times—could women who rejected matrimony, or who failed to marry for other reasons, become? Before the Enlightenment the main female alternative to matrimony was the nunnery: the woman had to be a bride—if not a man's, then Jesus's. Since the Enlightenment the role of the nunnery has been replaced in part by that of the madhouse or mental hospital: every woman still had to be in a domicile owned and controlled by a man or men —if not in her husband's home, then in a "mental home."

Demoralized by the spectacle of his mother's marriage, Hamlet orders Ophelia to the nunnery:

If thou dost marry, I'll give thee this plague for thy dowry: be thou as chaste as ice, as pure as snow, thou shall not escape calumny. Get thee to a nunnery. Go farewell.[16]

Demoralized by the spectacle of modern social life, Kallmann orders women to the madhouse. He advocates psychiatric incarceration as a systematic social policy on so-called eugenic grounds. "On a low cultural level," he explains, "the mentally deranged and feebleminded are barely able to obtain the necessities of life, while a high standard in the insane hospitals obviously tends to reduce the conditions inimical to the inmates." [17]

But this is not enough. The principal purpose of imprisoning schizophrenics, especially female schizophrenics, according to Kallmann, is to prevent them from marrying and procreating. In effect, he recommends mental hospitalization as a substitute for marriage:

On the other hand, confinement in an institution must exercise a definite influence on the reproductivity of the insane patient. Of course, such a purpose can only be accomplished if hospitalization takes place early enough, and is extended over the major part of the reproductive period in all hereditarily diseased patients. This point has been most often a neglected one, and even the more modern psychiatry still slights this important eugenic principle, to the detriment of the public health. It is merely necessary to recall that even today, girls in the first stages of schizophrenia (diagnosed very often as "nervousness") are not warned against early marriage, but rather are advised to marry as the best remedy for a "nervous breakdown." [18]

The practice of the principle Kallmann here proclaims—which was, of course, not his own invention but represented the opinion of the most prestigious heredity-obsessed psychiatrists of his time—is illustrated by the following story, reported in a daily newspaper:

Martha Nelson, who was committed to a state mental hospital for unknown reasons in 1875 at the age of 4 and spent the next 99 years in state institutions, died Thursday, according to the Ohio Department of Mental Health and Mental Retardation. She was 103 years old. . . . State officials said they were still not sure why Miss Nelson was confined all her life. She did laundry and housework . . . until she was 60 or 70, they said, staying on as a patient after that.[19]

To ask why this woman was "confined" at age sixty or seventy is to ask a question only in order to avoid an answer: namely, that the hospital was her home. Of course, that answer is ideologically insufficient. If one were asked in the Middle Ages why a woman had been living in a nunnery, the response could not be that she had no other place to stay; it would have to be that she did so because she loved Jesus. Similarly, we must now say that people live in mental hospitals not because they have no other place to stay, but because they are schizophrenic.

The proposition that the primary phenomenon in "madness" in the modern world—which became "dementia praecox" at the end of the nineteenth century and "schizophrenia" at the beginning of the twentieth—is forcible relocation from home to madhouse is borne out by the whole history of institutional psychiatry.[20] Even a cursory look at this history shows, and a more careful study of it amply confirms, that whatever the phenomenology of madness might have been in the past or might be today, confinement in a madhouse almost always came first, and its justification by madness came second.

Two hundred fifty years ago the English journalist and novelist Daniel Defoe denounced this practice as follows:

This leads me to exclaim against the vile Practice now so much in vogue among the better Sort, as they are called, but the worst sort in fact, namely, the sending their Wives to Mad-Houses at every Whim or Dislike, that they may be more secure and undisturb'd in their Debaucheries. . . . This is the height of Barbarity and Injustice in a Christian Country, it is a clandestine Inquisition, nay worse.[21]

But why did Englishmen do such terrible things to their wives? One reason was that they could not divorce them, a subject to which the greatest of all defenders of personal liberty, John Milton, had addressed himself—at about the same time that the building of insane asylums got under way—in the following remarkable words:

When, therefore, I perceived that there were three species of liberty which are essential to the happiness of social life—religious, domestic, and civil; and as I had already written concerning the first, and the magistrates were strenuously active in obtaining the third, I determined to turn my attention to the second or domestic species. . . . I explained my sentiments not only concerning the solemnization of marriage but the dissolution, if circumstances rendered it necessary; . . . for he in vain makes a vaunt of liberty in the senate or in the forum who languishes under the vilest servitude to an inferior at home. On this subject, therefore, I published some books which were more particularly necessary at that time, when man and wife were often the most inveterate foes, when the man often staid to take care of his children at home, while the mother of the family was seen in the camp of the enemy threatening death and destruction to her husband.[22]

The above was written in 1654. Within one hundred years, "lunacy" was a flourishing "trade" in England.[23] My point is not only that matrimony and psychiatry are similar institutions, but that they are interlinked and mutually supportive of one another. For example, an 1851 Illinois statute specified that married women could be compulsorily confined in the state insane asylum "at the request of the husband . . . without evidence of insanity required in other cases." [24]

In England the same principle was put into practice whenever the fact of marital infidelity was concealed by the fiction of mental illness—as, for example, in 1869, when the Prince of Wales, later Edward VII (popularly known as "Bertie") was threatened with scandal on account of his sexual liaison with a married woman. According to a modern biographer of the monarch:

> There was one more attempt to divert the scandal—by the loyal Sir Thomas Moncrieffe, the lady's father, who somewhat ruthlessly but patriotically had his daughter promptly declared insane. Leading doctors entered court to swear that she had been afflicted by "puerperal mania" after the birth of the child. This was accepted by the judge. . . . The judiciary had not exactly covered itself with glory, but the Queen's business had been done and Bertie rescued from a most unfortunate predicament.[25]

Thus, in proportion as matrimony is considered to be sacred and indissoluble, involuntary psychiatry will be considered to be blessed and indispensable; and insofar as marital discord and divorce are considered to be scandalous, mental illness and its compulsory treatment will be considered to be scientific.

We are ready now to reexamine, with the matrimonial model in mind, the actual context and the precise manner in which the phenomena that Kraepelin called "dementia praecox" and Bleuler called "schizophrenia" typically arise. The context is the family: parents and one or more children. The "affected" child is an adolescent, becoming a young adult, whose development (I will henceforth use the masculine pronoun for the sake of simplifying the presentation, although the "patient" is more often a woman *) seems to proceed in such a way as to give concern to the parents, and perhaps others, about his competence as an independent individual. He may be excessively childish and dependent on his parents, or excessively detached from them in a defiant show of illusory independence. In either case, his survival as an economically and personally independent adult, much less as the head of another household, seems increasingly doubtful. The subject—or "prepatient," as Goffman aptly calls him; [28] that is, our future schizophrenic patient—is now in his late teens, in the university, or perhaps just beyond it. Still, he remains economically dependent (on his family or others) and socially isolated (except from his family or a few others). Here, then, is the situation in which "schizophrenia" typically arises—that is, in which it is first "identified" or "diagnosed": aging parents, grown tired of looking after an offspring having reached biological maturity, are faced with the present burden and future prospect of supporting a "useless" and possibly "difficult" son or daughter. The questions that inevitably arise in their minds, and in the minds of other concerned family members, are: What will happen to this "child" when the parents become feeble and die? How will he live? Who will take care of him?

This is the situation in which we can observe dementia praecox or schizophrenia *in statu nascendi* (in its nascent

---

* At the Burghölzli Hospital during Bleuler's directorship, "Schizophrenic patients comprise[d] 71 per cent of the men and 79 per cent of the women patients. . . ." [26] Concerning the age of onset of this "disease" and its duration, Bleuler adds this significant remark: "Thus the social importance of schizophrenia is a tremendous one . . . because it affects most patients before they had the opportunity to establish themselves in life and work." [27] I have the impression that Bleuler actually realized that "schizophrenia" is the so-called schizophrenic's "life and work," but that he simply could not bring himself to say this and face the implications of saying it.

state). It is a situation, moreover, that resembles in all essentials the circumstances in which we can also observe (arranged) marriage *in statu nascendi*. As schizophrenia, or madness, two terms I shall use interchangeably, arises out of a context in which the prepatient plays a pivotal role, so marriage arises out of a context in which the prewife plays a pivotal role. By "prewife" I mean the young woman at the age and stage of life when she passes, imperceptibly, from child or adolescent into potential bride and wife; the age which revealingly used to be, and sometimes still is, called "marriageable."

What did people mean when they spoke of a young woman as "marriageable"? They meant that she ought *to get* married; that she ought *to be* married; that her father was ready *to give her away* in marriage. The existence or role that awaited such a person was that of wife; in short, she was a *prewife*. Then, as now, prewives were raised to be incompetent and useless as independent individuals outside of the home. They were expected to be unemployable in the market place, except perhaps at the lowest rungs of the economic and social ladder; instead, they were expected to be wives, mothers, and homemakers. I apologize for saying such obvious things, but my justification for doing so will emerge presently.

Having arrived at the age of marriageability, having become prewives, young women usually made their destiny their decision: they married and became wives. They were aided in effecting this change in their status by their families, by their prospective husbands' families, and often by go-betweens or marriage brokers. This is why the institution of matrimony functioned so well in the past, and functions so poorly now. Formerly, it met the needs of young women and their families, and the reciprocal needs of young men and their families. Now it is expected to meet the needs of the marriage partners as individuals, and this it fails to do.

In our day the structure and function of arranged marriage has been replaced in part by the structure and function of arranged psychiatry. It is important in this connection that the certification ceremony, which has many similarities to the wedding ceremony, is called "commitment"—a term that betrays the idea that not only is the patient committed to the hospital, but that patient and psychiatrist, like wife and husband, are also "committed" to each other.

The structural similarities between arranged marriage and arranged psychiatry are obvious enough. Sometimes the young prepatient seeks psychiatric help on his own and enters voluntarily into the psychiatric "matrimonial" bond which I shall describe more fully. More often, paralleling the pattern of arranged marriage, the task of bringing the prepatient together with his future psychiatric partner falls on the parents and other go-betweens, such as family physician, psychologist, social worker, and other so-called "mental health professionals." Having found a suitable medical match, prepatient and physician are readied for the certification ceremony: one of the participants is formally diagnosed as a "schizophrenic patient," the other is formally authenticated as "his psychiatric physician," and the space in which they are both confined, the one of course more tightly than the other, is formally accredited as a "hospital."

In short, as in holy matrimony the wife loses her name and takes the name her husband gives her, so in psychiatric matrimony the patient loses his name and takes the name his psychiatrist gives him. Thus does the marriage ceremony transform Joan Jones into Mrs. Steven Smith, identifying her henceforth as the "wife of Smith"; and thus does the commitment ceremony transform an accountant or architect into a schizophrenic, identifying him henceforth as "the patient of Dr. Daniel Doe."

Moreover, this institutional psychiatric arrangement, like its matrimonial counterpart, is also ready-made for the disposition of certain common human problems. Hence, not only are the participants in this drama spared the need of newly creating this (psychiatric) solution for their problems, but, on the contrary, they are pushed along, with all the pressure society can exert, toward resolving their particular needs in this way. Parents and society need caretakers for certain persons who—because of their upbringing, education, or whatever other reason—cannot or do not want to be self-caring. Such persons are, moreover, usually willing to accept, especially when faced with authoritative pressure and coercion to do so, certain people and institutions other than their parents and families as their supporters and caretakers.

As in the arranged pairing of patriarchal marriage, so in the arranged pairing of hospitalized schizophrenic and hospital psychiatrist, there may be no courtship at all: the first time patient and doctor meet may be in the hospital, after the former has been committed to the "care" of the latter. Committed by a judge, neither patient nor doctor is free to reject the union, at least not out of hand. As in the matrimonial model, it is obvious, however, that the hospital psychiatrist has the necessary power, should he wish to use it, both to initiate such a union—that is, to bring certain patients into the hospital and under his care—and to terminate such a union—that is, to discharge, as cured or in remission, virtually any patient he wishes. What is perhaps most revealing in this connection is that despite the much-vaunted medical model on which psychiatry is ostensibly based, this sort of psychiatric arrangement lacks the most distinguishing political characteristic of medicine—namely, the free choice of physician by the patient, and vice versa. In short, while the modern medical relationship aspires to the model of the romantic marriage or love-match, freely entered into by two consenting parties choosing one another, the modern psychiatric relationship aspires to the model of traditional marriage, arranged for the partners by the superiors of their respective clans.

Thus, some of the functions of social differentiation and identification formerly discharged by the institution of matrimony are now discharged by the institution of psychiatry. In every society everyone has his or her "proper place"—and is, more or less rigidly, kept in it. Although this is more true for traditional stratified societies than it is for modern, seemingly classless ones, the maintenance, over certain periods of time at least, of relatively fixed social roles is a characteristic of all societies.

In the patriarchal societies of Europe until the turn of the century, and beyond, the woman's place was, in the classic German phrase, *Kinder, Kirche, Küche* (children, church, kitchen). As women—and other oppressed groups, such as the Jews, the workers, and the poor—became "liberated," and as societies became seemingly classless, new subject classes arose: the mentally ill form one such class, while welfare recipients, children, and the physically handicapped are some of the others. Now it is the members of these groups that must know, and be kept in, their proper places. The schizophrenic's "place" has been defined by Bleuler: loosening of associations, autism, and ambivalence. The alliterative "three A's," the classic "primary symptoms of schizophrenia," have thus replaced the alliterative "three K's," the classic "primary symptoms of femininity."

The course, prognosis, and eventual outcome of schizophrenia may also be profitably viewed from the perspective of the paradigm of arranged marriage. The characteristic age of onset of dementia praecox is, as we have seen, the same as that at which young women used to be, and still are, expected to get married. The characteristic expectations—familial and social, medical and psychiatric—of Victorian prewives and Bleulerian preschizophrenics are also the same: incompetence outside of the home, dependency on authority and family, unemployability in the market place.

Once committed (married), the patients (wives) are expected to have a lifelong disease (remain married till death parts them from their husbands). Sometimes the schizophrenic patient has a remission, is discharged from the hospital, and returns to his premorbid personality (the husband gets a divorce and the ex-wife returns to her parental home). Often, however, the ex-patient suffers a relapse and is rehospitalized (the ex-wife remarries). From this perspective, it would be as false and misleading to say that schizophrenia is a chronic condition as it would be to say that being a dutiful wife is a chronic condition. It would be more accurate to attribute chronicity to certain social expectations and institutional arrangements than to the "conditions" they generate. Of course, marriage lasts a long time if divorce is prohibited by law or impeded by severe social sanctions. Of course, schizophrenia lasts a long time if recovery from it is prohibited by psychiatry or impeded by severe social sanctions. In Italy, for example, there was until recently no divorce; wives could escape from husbands, and vice versa, only by annulment or separation. Similarly, in Kraepelinian-Bleulerian-Freudian psychiatry, there was no recovery from schizophrenia; patients had a choice between escaping from their doctors or settling for a remission, and psychiatrists had a choice between rejecting hospital psychiatry and reclassifying "cured" schizophrenics as misdiagnosed neurotics.

In marriage the prewife gains a husband to replace her father, and a new home and family—all of which enable her to live as "wife" and "homemaker." Similarly, in mental hospitalization the prepatient gains a doctor to replace his father, and a new home and institution to replace his former home and family —all of which enable him to live as a patient and help run the institution. Thus, not only is schizophrenia a "way of life"; it is also a part of a social arrangement and institution that defines and offers a certain way of life—namely, institutional psychiatry. Here the patient is, as it were, the wife; the psychiatrist is the husband; the mental hospital is the home in which they both live; "schizophrenic" is the unflattering name by which the husband calls the wife; "doctor" is the flattering name by which the wife calls the husband; and the mental hospital inmates, especially those even more helpless than the patient himself, are the other children for whom mother and father—the "schizophrenic who has made an institutional recovery" and the "mental hospital director"—care together, the former doing all of the work, and the latter reaping all of the rewards for it.

The results of long years of forced psychiatric matrimony are generally the same as those of long years of holy matrimony: both doctor and patient develop deep-seated grievances against each other. And each has his own imagery and rhetoric to justify his complaints. Thus, on the one side stand the psychiatrists, fearful of patients, always ready to prove that the "psychotic" may be dangerous to himself or others and hence a fit subject for involuntary mental hospitalization and treatment. On the other side stand the patients, resentful of psychiatrists, always ready to claim that they have been treated unfairly and improperly and have, as a result, suffered indignities and injuries for which they are entitled to compensation. This is why, just as in litigations for divorce a judge or jury can always find fault with one party or another or both, depending on their own values and sympathies, so in litigations between psychiatric partners a judge or jury can always find fault with one party or another or both; and why those arbitrating such matters—that is, whether to commit patients or to compensate them —can, depending on the skill of the protagonists in this drama, easily justify actions for or against either patients or psychiatrists. It is difficult to see how it could be otherwise: insofar as human, especially paired, relationships are coerced rather than contracted, there will always be a need to justify both the coercion and the claim that it is abused, and it will always require a veritable Solomon to arbitrate such disputes.

From this perspective it is easy to see, too, why one of the most popular symptoms of the Victorian wife was frigidity— that is, she was sexually unresponsive to the husband she did not want and to whom she refused to submit; and why one of the characteristic symptoms of the contemporary schizophrenic is resistance to treatment—that is, he is therapeutically unresponsive to the psychiatrist he does not want and to whom he refuses to submit.

In many essential respects, then, hospital psychiatry—as it developed in eighteenth- and nineteenth-century Europe, and as we now know it throughout the "civilized" world—is a perfect replica of the "happy" Victorian marriage. It is stable—the patient is chronically psychotic, and the psychiatrist chronically psychiatric. It is peaceful—power is distributed and secured in a tight vertical network, thus eliminating both the possibility of effective revolt by the oppressed and of effective reform by the oppressor. It is animated and governed by nothing but love and goodwill—everything that the patient must do constitutes receiving treatment, and everything that the psychiatrist does constitutes giving treatment. Finally, just as holy matrimony produces nothing if not marital bliss, so psychiatric commitment produces nothing if not mental health.

We must keep in mind, however—and now I am quite serious—that neither the matrimonial nor the madness system was created by society to make its members happy or healthy. Each system serves a quite different purpose, and those who want to be happy or healthy must find their own way to attain their goals, within the system or outside of it.

Countless modern novelists and playwrights, from Ibsen and Chekhov to Pinter and Mishima, have wrestled with the problematic relations such as we have surveyed between prescribed pairs, whether matrimonial or psychiatric. A few citations from, and remarks on, literary works should suffice here to amplify and clarify my argument.

Tolstoy, much of whose life—both personal and creative—

was a gigantic struggle to exorcise the demons of domination-submission in human affairs,[29] saw to the heart of this problem not only as it affects marriage, but also as it affects medicine as a method of mystifying it. Here is a fragment of a dialogue from *The Kreutzer Sonata*. It is part of a conversation on a train between a man just released from prison for killing his wife and his anonymous interlocutor:

> "You know," he began while packing the tea and sugar into his bag, "the domination of women from which the world suffers all arises from this." "What domination of women?" I asked. "The rights, the legal privileges, are all on the man's side." "Yes, yes! That's just it," he interrupted me. "That's just what I want to say. It explains the extraordinary phenomenon that on the one hand woman is reduced to the lowest stage of humiliation, while on the other she dominates. . . . Woman's lack of rights arises not from the fact that she must not vote or be a judge—to be occupied with such affairs is no privilege—but from the fact that she is not man's equal in sexual intercourse and has not the right to use a man or abstain from him as she likes—is not allowed to choose a man at her pleasure instead of being chosen by him. . . . As it is at present, a woman is deprived of that right while a man has it." [30]

If we substitute psychiatrist for man and schizophrenic for woman, the fit is still perfect: The one can choose, or "diagnose," the other, but not vice versa.

Tolstoy bewails the mutual entrapment of men and women as slave-owners and slaves, and characterizes "the majority of women" as condemned to being "mentally diseased, hysterical, unhappy, and lacking capacity for spiritual development." [31] He then makes this prophetic observation about the role of physicians in demoralizing and mystifying this quintessentially ethical dilemma of mankind:

"I see you don't like doctors," I said, noticing a peculiarly malevolent tone in his voice whenever he alluded to them.

"It is not a case of liking or disliking. They have ruined my life as they have ruined and are ruining the lives of thousands and hundreds of thousands of human beings, and I cannot help connecting the effect with the cause. . . . Today one can no longer say: 'You are not living rightly, live better.' One can't say that, either to oneself or to anyone else. If you live a bad life, it is caused by the abnormal functioning of your nerves. So you must go to them, and they will prescribe eight penn'orth of medicine from a chemist, which you must take! You get still worse: then more medicine and the doctor again. An excellent trick!" [32]

This, surely, is a prescient perspective on the modern psychopharmacological management of marital and other human problems. It is extended in the following passage, in which Tolstoy also offers a dramatic description of the marital—and, *mutatis mutandis,* the psychiatric—imprisonment of each partner by the other:

Those new theories of hypnotism, psychic disease, and hysterics are not a simple folly, but a dangerous and repulsive one. Charcot would certainly have said that my wife was hysterical, and that I was abnormal, and he would no doubt have tried to cure me. But there was nothing to cure. Thus we lived in a perpetual fog, not seeing the condition we were in. . . . We were like two convicts hating each other and chained together, poisoning one another's lives and trying not to see it. I did not then know that ninety-nine per cent of married people live in a similar hell to the one I was in and that it cannot be otherwise.[33]

In *Natural Enemies,* Julius Horwitz has produced a stunning contemporary sequel to *The Kreutzer Sonata.* This novel is, in fact, an even more perceptive analysis of marriage as a trap for both husband and wife—partly, perhaps, because marriage is even more problematic now than it was in Tolstoy's day. Moreover, Horwitz is exceedingly critical of psychiatry's pernicious influence on those struggling to loosen or sever the bonds of matrimony. "The psychologists are wrong," Horwitz remarks in an aside similar to Tolstoy's on Charcot, "as they usually are. The professions in America are not generally concerned with being right but only in protecting the knowledge they feel comfortable with—like the psychiatrists who still don't realize Freud was a great fiction writer." [34]

Horwitz's protagonist is a successful editor who lives in the suburbs with his wife, children, and dog. As Tolstoy's story is told by a man who had killed his wife and served his time for it in prison, Horwitz's is told by a man who is planning to kill his wife, children, and himself, and who does so at the novel's end. In both cases marriage is an existential prison. "It made no difference," explains the husband, "that I edited one of the most important magazines in America according to *Newsweek,* Miriam saw me as a man who interfered with a private image of herself that she was utterly incapable of making clear to herself or anyone else." [35]

Miriam "goes mad," tries suicide, becomes a mental hospital patient and then a psychiatric outpatient, making her husband guilty and resentful. "Why women chose madness was beyond my comprehension," [36] Horwitz has him saying in anger and desperation, while showing us that he understands it only too well. Husband and wife have trapped each other, and themselves, in a marriage they will not examine, much less dissolve, and which the psychiatrists who treat Miriam distract them from examining or dissolving.

This, then, is the problem that becomes psychiatrized, with disastrous results. "I am mad, of course, the hospital records show it," [37] says Miriam. While Horwitz spares us a formal diagnosis, Miriam's madness is clearly what any red-blooded American psychiatrist would call schizophrenia. As the story nears its climax, Miriam senses her husband's unappeasable resentment. It is too late, but at last she communicates her grievances to her husband in words rather than symptoms:

> Psychiatrists don't like people, they prefer patients. You never fought him. You seemed to accept his judgments when you must have known they were wrong. You should have taken me out of the hospital before the electric shocks. I don't believe I was ever mentally ill.[38]

Miriam's husband knows she is right. He always knew it. But they both went along, she playing the role of suffering patient, he that of supportive husband. Horwitz's final comments on psychiatrists, put in the husband's mouth, are most telling:

> The psychiatrist who put Miriam on Ritalin, then Thorazine, then Valium, committed suicide by jumping in front of a northbound Lexington Avenue subway train. He fell across the tracks and his head and limbs were partly decapitated as though he had been guillotined by a madman. Psychiatrists led gynecologists in the number of deaths by suicide.[39]

If Tolstoy and Horwitz—and Chekhov, Kraus, and Kesey— write like this about psychiatry, perhaps they know something to which people should pay more attention. In *Natural Enemies* Horwitz captures with perfect fidelity the modern "dynamic" psychiatrist's determination to destroy the last vestiges of his "patient's" sense of self as a moral agent,* a sense already self-impaired by the "patient" himself:

---

* Modern writers are given to rediscovering that "alienists" are usually alienated from themselves and their society, and that if their clients suffer from anomie, they usually make them more, rather than less, anomic.

I should have dragged Miriam away from the Seventy-fourth Street psychiatrist. He gave Miriam a false language that left out verbs. . . . She became a part of the madness Freud created like other madmen before him who believed they have stumbled on the meaning of life. . . . Psychiatry would die out like the practice of letting blood did.[40]

It may seem like a long way from Czarist Russia or from contemporary America to Japan after World War II, where Mishima wrote *Forbidden Colors* (*Kinjiki*). Yet, Tolstoy's, Horwitz's, and Mishima's ideas and sentiments are similar, showing us the universality of the "problem" of man's and woman's "proper place" vis-à-vis one another and in the social order. Here, first, are Mishima's remarks on the pressure to conform to the prescribed pairing of marriage:

When a girl appears who loves you as much as Yasuko seems to [says Shunsuké to Yuichi], it would seem best to marry her, since you have to get married sometime. Don't take marriage as being anything more than a triviality. It's trivial —that's why they call it sacred.[41]

Then follow Mishima's observations about the necessity to keep the woman in her place—lest, the implication is clear, she inverts the pattern of domination-submission and overwhelms the man:

[Yuichi]: "But how can someone get married if he doesn't want to?"
[Shunsuké]: "I'm not joking. Men marry logs; they can even marry ice boxes. Marriage is man's own invention. It is something he can do; desire isn't necessary. . . . The only thing to be careful about is never to acknowledge at any time that she [the wife] has a soul. Even the dregs of a soul are out of the question here." [42]

Here, again, we may replace man by hospital psychiatrist, and woman by hospitalized schizophrenic, and the fit remains perfect. What the tradition of Kraepelinian, organic, hospital psychiatry forbids is recognition of the patient as a person. The psychiatrist's penalty for lapsing from this principle, and the conduct it prescribes, is set forth movingly by Chekhov in *Ward No. 6.*[43] So as not to digress further I shall not quote from this, but I would like to conclude with one more passage from *Forbidden Colors,* in which Mishima drives home the moral cost, in the contemporary world, of the institution of arranged marriage, and, *mutatis mutandis,* of institutional psychiatry:

> These [Shunsuké's] two hands and nothing else had awakened in him [Yuichi] a passion for forced marriages, vice, phoniness and falsehood, and had induced him to embrace them. These two hands were close to death, had formed a secret alliance with death.[44]

Shunsuké's hands are Kraepelin's, and Bleuler's, and Freud's. It is time that we stopped clasping them in a friendly handshake.

If marriage is a trap that often ends in divorce to free those held captive by it, why do men and women so often remarry? And if psychiatric commitment is a trap that often ends unhappily for both inmate and keeper, why do patients and psychiatrists so often recreate the same sort of situation? There are two obvious reasons for this. First, both the matrimonial and the psychiatric roles exert powerful attractions on people generally, and on mental patients and psychiatrists particularly; they are also careers that define the very identities of husbands and wives, psychiatrists and psychotics, and are, therefore, difficult to relinquish. Second, through the marriage contract, matrimony offers a means of controlling the man-woman relationship that other, less formal, less coercive arrangements lack; similarly, through commitment, institutional psychiatry offers a means of controlling the psychiatrist-patient relationship that other, less formal, less coercive arrangements lack. Without such a legally binding contract—literally, a mutual "commitment"—men and women, psychiatrists and patients, can separate with relative ease, and often do so. Hence, those who desire marital or psychiatric security—for reasons that range over the whole gamut of human needs—will explicitly opt for marriage or tacitly choose psychiatric commitment.

In a fine article on divorce and remarriage, Sonya O'Sullivan describes a woman's progress from liberated sex partner to licensed second wife:

> Muriel is caught up in a paradoxical situation. Having persuaded Mr. that marriage is stultifying, an obsolete institution, she finds that she very much wants to be married to him. Having discoursed, quite brilliantly, on the development of The Home into a monument to a dead relationship, she finds that she very much wants a home, with Mr. securely in it. Having uttered enticingly racy comments on the subject of fidelity, she insists that Mr. be faithful. And, having pointed out the preposterousness of Mrs.'s expecting to be supported financially, it has occurred to her that her tiny income hardly justifies her working from nine till five (after they are married), and when Mr.'s tax bracket is taken into consideration, it would actually save money to stay home. It is a paradox but not a problem.[45]

The point, of course, is that one cannot simultaneously maximize freedom and security, independence from matrimony or psychiatry, and also avow dependence on these institutions. That is, one cannot have one's cake and eat it, too. Or can one? Current marital and psychiatric trends seem to me to demand just such an interpretation—that is, as attempts sequentially to maximize both members of a pair of internally contradictory human needs and social practices.

In another article, mainly on second marriages, Leslie Westoff reports that, in the United States, second marriages end in divorce almost twice as often as first ones, current figures being 59 percent for the former and 37 percent for the latter.[46] Present trends in marriage, divorce, and remarriage rates are closely paralleled by current trends in mental hospital admission, discharge, and readmission rates. Protracted stay in the mental hospital, necessitated supposedly by schizophrenic "deterioration," has decreased dramatically. In fact, many psychiatrists—even the authors of psychiatric textbooks—now admit that this stage of the "illness" is an artifact created by chronic institutionalization.[47] However, rates for first admission to mental hospitals, like those for first marriages, continue to be high, while discharge rates, like rates for divorce, are also increasing. At the same time, rates for readmissions to mental hospitals, as for remarriages, remain high and may be increasing; but these rehospitalizations often end in discharge, just as remarriages often end in divorce. All this suggests an uneasy compromise between a continuing craving for both marital and psychiatric security and for freedom from the bonds that such security entails. "Underlying all our difficulties with marriage," remarks Westoff in a phrase that is at once true and trite, "is certainly a desire for freer, more realistic and equal relationships, unfettered by legal contract." [48] In other words, the desire is for a relationship that is, in any conventional sense of the term, not a marriage at all. For what is marriage without legal compulsion? What is schizophrenia without legal commitment? What, to vary the metaphor, is a triangle without three sides?

It seems to me that just as a wholly voluntary relationship between man and woman negates the very concept of marriage, so a wholly voluntary relationship between psychiatrist and patient negates the concept of schizophrenia (in the usual sense of this term). Or, to put it differently, I would suggest that involuntary or institutional psychiatry is to voluntary or contractual psychiatry [49] as marriage is to an affair. The former locks the partners together in a tight embrace of ambivalence and law; the latter links them together in a loose union of affection and convenience. This is why puritanical persons regard men who marry women as virtuous—because they willingly shoulder their "moral responsibility" toward them; and regard those who shun marriage as wicked—because they "refuse to accept their moral responsibility" toward helpless women. Similarly, this is why puritanical psychiatrists regard physicians who commit mental patients as virtuous—because they willingly shoulder their "medical responsibility" toward them; and regard those who shun commitment as wicked—because they "refuse to accept their medical responsibility" toward "desperately ill mental patients."

Inevitably, the relationship between the partners in both holy and psychiatric matrimony is often mutually constraining personally, and ambivalent emotionally.* Like the dependent wife needing the despotic husband and vice versa, the schizophrenic patient needs the hospital psychiatrist, and vice versa, each being unable—because of the combined weight of shame and

* It is worth noting in this connection that in American slang, the two most common vulgar terms for sexual intercourse—namely, "fuck" and "screw," both of which are used in the sense of the male doing "it" to the female—also mean cheating or taking advantage of someone. Homely language thus reflects more honestly than does technical language the frequently exploitative nature of the sexual, and marital, relationship. These terms are now also commonly applied to the psychiatric relationship by those who disapprove of the psychiatrist's uncontrolled power over his patient.

guilt, medical mystification and social hypocrisy—to acknowledge his or her need for, and exploitation of, the other. Instead of mutual need, each feels and talks about help—one wanting to receive it, the other to give it. Instead of mutual exploitation, each feels and talks about lack of understanding and unjustified antagonism—the patient about the psychiatrist's, the psychiatrist about the patient's. In short, schizophrenia is the tip of an iceberg: below the water level lies the "bad marriage" of psychotic and psychiatrist, each partner bitterly dissatisfied with the other, but each choosing to sustain, rather than to sever, the relationship.

On the map which the metaphor of marriage provides for the so-called problem of schizophrenia, one area stands out with special clarity. I refer to the fact that, in the United States as well as in many other countries, a person could not, until a few decades ago, be admitted to a state (or similar public) mental hospital voluntarily, that is, because he wanted to become a patient; nor could a psychiatrist admit such a person as a patient, that is, because he wanted to hospitalize him. Admission to such a mental institution, as to a penal institution, could be gained through court action only. Being a mental hospital patient then meant being committed to the hospital; being a doctor vis-à-vis such a patient meant being assigned to him by a judge or by one's hospital superiors.

Obviously, this arrangement resembles nothing at all in the practice of medicine in free societies. It resembles, besides the arrangement governing induction into the roles of prisoner and warden, the arrangement governing induction into the roles of involuntary wife and husband—which, in American slang, is called a "shotgun wedding." In such a wedding, man and woman marry under the threat of being killed, typically by the woman's father who, under the guise of protecting his family's honor, actually wants to get rid of the burden which his daughter is to him. Civil commitment is also a "shotgun wedding": it unites, in the matrimony of madness, psychotic and psychiatrist under the threat of the irresistible coercion of society, typically exercised through the order of a judge who, under the guise of protecting the public safety and the patient's mental health, actually wants to get rid of the burden which the madman is to him.

It is important to keep in mind that just as in a shotgun wedding both the bride and groom are coerced, so in civil commitment both psychotic and psychiatrist are coerced; neither is free to reject the roles assigned to him and his partner, or the relationship between them assigned to both. This account demonstrates clearly the precise social mechanism by which both schizophrenia and psychiatry are, almost literally, created or manufactured: [50] through the collaboration of all the major social institutions of society—law and medicine, religion and the family, education and journalism—the courts define some persons as "insane" or "psychotic," some others as "sane" or "psychiatrist," the relationship between them as "hospitalization" and "treatment," and then impose these definitions and roles on them by fraud, force, and the lures of protection and prestige.

This kind of psychiatric pairing—which was virtually the only kind that existed until late in the nineteenth century, when the practice of certain kinds of voluntary relationships between psychiatric patients and psychiatrists first arose—had the advantage which blatant brutality has over covert coercion: at least it made it crystal clear that patient and doctor, psychotic and psychiatrist did not choose each other. Like wife and husband in arranged marriages, they knew they had to get along but did not have to love each other. Each could therefore retreat into his own role and could, by and large, be left in peace by the other: the patient could occupy himself with his psychosis, the doctor with his diagnosis. This accounted both for the stability and the course of the relationship: the patient "deteriorated" by becoming steadily better at being psychotic; the psychiatrist "developed" by becoming steadily better at being psychiatric.

The delicate balance of this idyllic marital arrangement was upset by the introduction into institutional psychiatry of the notion that the psychotic patient was supposed to receive, and the psychiatrist was supposed to give, something more than room and board and perhaps some guidance, called "custodial care and moral treatment." Beginning with the success of malaria treatment for paresis in 1917, and gathering momentum with the introduction, in the 1930s, of insulin treatment for schizophrenia, the "medical treatment" of this "disease," too, was supposed to be "active" and "aggressive." In other words, the unhappy couple was now expected to copulate—and to enjoy it! The result was the horrifying institutionalization of psychiatric rape—that is, the "therapeutic attacks" of the psychiatrist on the psychotic, through metrazol, insulin, electricity, lobotomy, and psychopharmacology.

Then, just as the bonds of holy matrimony were loosened in the twentieth century, so were the bonds of psychiatric matrimony. One manifestation of this new "permissiveness" was that the marriage partners were sometimes allowed to choose and reject each other; another was that after being united in matrimony, they could, if sufficiently motivated, divorce each other. These changes resulted in several new developments in both psychiatry and schizophrenia. For example, it became possible for a prepatient to choose to enter a public mental hospital voluntarily; this, in turn, made it possible for him—first in principle, then in practice—to choose to leave it. Marriage Italian or Catholic style became, in other words, marriage American or Protestant style: divorce became possible and often even relatively easy, and so, often, did discharge from the mental hospital.

However, just as easing the divorce laws has not destroyed the institution of marriage, but, on the contrary, has in some ways strengthened it, so easing the possibilities of divorce between hospitalized psychotic and hospital psychiatrist has not destroyed institutional psychiatry, but, on the contrary, has in some ways strengthened it. Without divorce or with it, marriage and fornication have remained distinct concepts and values; the institution of marriage has remained legally protected and socially esteemed. With compulsory commitment of the insane or without it, madness and sanity, psychiatric cure and personal conversation have remained distinct concepts and values; the institution of psychiatry has remained legally protected and socially esteemed. The result is that just as following divorce there remain ex-wives and ex-husbands who frequently feel comfortable only after establishing new bonds of matrimony, so following psychiatric discharge from a mental hospital there remain ex-mental patients and hospital psychiatrists who frequently feel comfortable only after establishing new bonds of psychiatric matrimony. In short, we have the typical contemporary Western psychiatric scene: prepatients and ex-patients in desperate search of psychiatrists who will make them well (happy), and psychiatrists in equally desperate search of patients whom they can save from mental illness (being unmarried).

Only in this light—that is, by viewing the schizophrenic (or sometimes his relatives) as seeking a better psychiatrist, which is a wholly post-Kraepelinian and post-Bleulerian phenomenon, and so closely resembles the search of the unhappily married or recently divorced woman seeking a better husband (and vice versa)—can we understand certain novel features of modern psychiatry. Perhaps the most striking among these is the appearance and disappearance, often in quick succession, of promises of a new cure for schizophrenia (and other psychoses), each linked to the name of an ambitious and mendacious psychiatrist. These psychiatrists, armed with their new "treatments"—which they offer to add to the "armamentarium" of other psychiatric methods—promise to cure the schizophrenic, thus restoring, in one fell swoop, not only his mental health, but also his (and everyone else's) faith in psychiatric matrimony. Harry Stack Sullivan, Frieda Fromm-Reichmann, Marguerite Sechehaye, John Rosen, and Ronald Laing are among the best-known figures who have promised to effect cures of schizophrenia where others have failed; who, in other words, are like the man who promises a woman unhappily married once, twice, or several times, true happiness in a new marriage—to him. But this kind of therapeutic seduction is just that; although I have no wish to deny that some psychiatrists may be more helpful to their clients than some others, I want to emphasize that what they can accomplish cannot exceed the bounds set by their own roles as "therapists" and the roles of their partners as "patients." To put it bluntly but simply, as wives cannot recover from marriage so long as they have husbands, so mental patients cannot recover from psychosis (or any other mental illness) so long as they have psychiatrists.

This interdependence between husbands and wives, psychiatrists and mental patients—so baneful for the personal independence of each, and so beneficial for matrimony and psychiatry—is now becoming more widely appreciated. This, I think, is why there are now, more than ever before in history, profound and increasingly pervasive doubts about matrimony and psychiatry—among both men and women, both psychiatrists and patients. Women's liberationists have reemphasized the age-old oppression of women by men, but they have had the courage to go beyond it, to acknowledge that women have exploited their positions as slaves, and that the only way to overcome their subjection is by both economic and personal independence from men. This means that women should not be expected to be supported by men as wives, but must support themselves by work salable in the marketplace. Similarly, mental-patient liberationists have reemphasized the age-old oppression of institutionalized mental patients by institutional psychiatrists, but they, too, have had the courage to go beyond it, to acknowledge that mental patients have exploited their positions as slaves, and that the only way to overcome their subjection is by both economic and personal independence from psychiatrists. This means that "psychotics" should not expect to be supported by psychiatrists (society) as patients, but must support themselves by work salable in the marketplace. To the extent that women and "psychotics" cannot, or do not, so liberate themselves, they will remain enslaved to men who "love" them and to psychiatrists who "treat" them.

The appositeness of the paradigm of marriage to the problems of medicine, and especially of psychiatry, is revealed dramatically by the recent metamorphosis of both the marital and the medical relationship: during the past century, arranged marriages have been transformed into marriages chosen by the partners, and medical pairings chosen by the partners have been transformed into arranged medical "marriages."

In Victorian Europe among the middle and upper classes, it would have been unthinkable that the medical relationship could be imposed on either patient or doctor. "Free choice of physician" by the patient was the sacred symbol of medicine as a "free profession," while its corollary, free choice of patient by the physician (except under certain special emergency conditions), was too obvious to be articulated. At the same time and among the same classes, it would have been equally unthinkable that the marriage relationship could be based on the free choice of the partners. Marriage, people generally believed, was an institution that affects countless individuals, indeed all of society, not only the prospective wife and husband; it would be wrong, therefore, to leave the selection of suitable mates in the hands of the partners alone. In particular, marriage affected the bride's father, who provided her dowry. Since the young woman did not finance her marriage, how could she, and why should she, be left free to decide whom to marry? Is it not reasonable to let him who pays the piper call the tune, or at least have a say about which tunes are acceptable? Finally, people believed—and who can blame them?—that the choice of a suitable marriage partner was too difficult a task to be left to persons so young and inexperienced as prospective wives and husbands usually were.

We now regard these arguments in support of arranged marriage as antiquated and absurd, and pride ourselves on our "emancipation" and "modernity" in having adopted as our moral ideal of marriage the paradigm of free choice by the partners. We seem quite unaware that we have actually exchanged arranged marital pairings for arranged medical pairings. For although we now believe in free choice of marriage partners, we no longer believe in free choice of medical partners. In both free and totalitarian societies, we have thus come to accept the paradigm of medical pairing pioneered by psychiatry—that is, pairing prescribed by professional, legal, and societal authorities, rather than created by the personal choice of the participants themselves. The contemporary explanation and justification for this arranged medicine is, moreover, exactly the same as the explanation and justification for arranged marriage had been a century ago.

Medicine, so this "explanation" runs, is an institution that affects countless people besides patient and doctor; hence, it would be wrong to leave the medical relationship to be freely determined by these two parties. Specifically, the medical relationship affects employers, insurance carriers, and the state, who often pay for hospital care and the physician's services; how, then, can these parties be excluded from having a say in it? Moreover, it is now widely believed that the choice of medical partners is too difficult a task to be left to the partners alone. The patient is too ignorant and the physician too greedy;

the former is too gullible and the latter too likely to gull him. It is best, therefore, that, like bride and groom in days gone by, patient and doctor be assigned to each other by their betters. The practice of institutional psychiatry, and of medicine generally, has thus been increasingly shaped by legislatures, courts, and insurance companies. Illustrative examples abound: abortion is a state-prohibited crime one day and a state-supported treatment the next; birth control pills and cigarettes are deemed safe, while cyclamates and Laetrile are not; taking heroin is a disease, but taking methadone is a treatment.[51]

The result of these momentous cultural and economic changes has been a complete metamorphosis, during the past century, of both the marital and medical relationships—the one shifting from arranged to free pairing, the other from free to arranged pairing.* This exchange between the patterning of matrimonial and medical matings has been the most complete in Soviet Russia, and the most sudden in post-World War II Japan. A few brief remarks on each should help to amplify our understanding of these profound social changes.

Until the advent of communism in 1917, Russian marriages conformed to the traditional pattern developed in feudal Europe, and were, of course, under the strict control of the Russian Orthodox Church. Marriage was arranged, the husband had tyrannical powers over the wife, and there was no divorce. At the same time, medicine, insofar as it was available, was a service dispensed on the model of untrammeled capitalism: those who could afford medical services could purchase them as they might any other service; those who could not had a choice between doing without such services or accepting them as a charity. Medicine was thus free, not in the modern sense of such services being made available to people under the auspices and control of the state, but in the old-fashioned sense of

---

* The implications of these changes—on matters ranging from grounds for divorce to grounds for malpractice—are far-reaching but beyond the scope of this inquiry.

the relationship being freely initiated and freely terminated by both patient and physician.

With the abolition of private property and the free market, the most powerful ideological motives of communism were rallied behind the destruction of both the arranged marriage and the capitalist mode of providing medical care. Both marriage and divorce were removed from clerical and put under civil authority. The marriage pattern was thus transformed from arrangement by parents and relatives to self-selection by the partners. The rules for divorce, now squarely in the hands of the state, were relaxed, but the actual availability of divorce varied from time to time, depending on the family policies pursued by the communist rulers.

Paralleling this change in the matrimonial relationship, the medical relationship was removed from the private sector and put under the watchful eye of the state, much as marriage had been under that of the church. Free choice by patient and physician became as much of an absurdity under communism as free choice by prospective wife and husband had been under Russian Christianity. In short, Russian marriages used to be arranged and are now free, whereas Russian medicine used to be free and is now arranged. The medical relationship can be initiated or terminated, by both patient and physician, only if it is arranged and authorized by their superiors (who are bureaucratic agents of the state), or if they can justify to them their own desire to do so.

In Japan, both traditional marital and psychiatric practices remained relatively stable until after World War II. Then they both changed dramatically. According to Landis, among all of the countries in the modern world, "The greatest shift from arranged marriages to some other type came about after World War II in Japan, where previously all marriages had been arranged." [52] This change correlates amazingly closely with the massive and rapid spread in that country during the same time of the principles and practices of institutional psychiatry.

Traditionally, the care of so-called mental patients in Japan was, as I mentioned earlier, not a medical but a family matter.[53] The so-called "law of private imprisonment" [54]—a revealing term, indeed—empowered families to confine some of their members in "cells" in their own homes, where they were looked after, well or badly as the case might be, by relatives and servants. It was, in effect, an informal and nonmedical system of "psychiatric" care and control. Although Japanese medicine came under the influence of Kraepelinian psychiatry early in the twentieth century, it was not until after World War II that it became thoroughly westernized and medicalized. As Masaki Kato explains:

> Along with the development of industrialization and urbanization in Japan, psychiatric patients became excluded from their families and society, and the number of psychiatric beds has been increasing rapidly; i.e., four beds per 10,000 in 1954, to 25 in 1972, which means an increase of more than six times in psychiatric beds per population.[55]

It is especially significant that this tremendous increase in psychiatric beds occurred in Japan precisely during the period when the number of hospitalized mental patients in Western countries, especially in the United States, decreased precipitously, in some states by 50 percent or more.

It is generally contended by Western psychiatrists that the decrease in mental hospital patients in their countries is due to the therapeutic effectiveness of the phenothiazines, which were introduced into psychiatry in the 1950s. However, since these drugs have also been widely used in Japan, this claim is unconvincing, to say the least. It seems clear that psychiatric pairings between psychotics and psychiatrists, just as matrimonial pairings between wives and husbands, are so profoundly affected, indeed regulated, by the economic, legal, and social contexts in which they occur that it would be as foolish to attribute increased rates of discharges from mental hospitals to Thorazine as it would be to attribute increased rates of divorce to Valium.

The matrimonial model of the madness network which I am proposing seems to me to be an indispensable tool for dispelling our current psychiatric confusions about schizophrenia. As we now recognize that mating is both the cause and consequence of the wife-husband relationship or holy matrimony, so we should also recognize that madness is both the cause and consequence of the psychotic-psychiatrist relationship or psychiatric matrimony.

In some societies mating outside of matrimony is prohibited and is called, for example, "fornication." Similarly, in some societies madness outside of the madhouse is prohibited and is called, for example, "dangerousness to self and others." The fact that both of these types of acts—that is, both "fornication" and "dangerousness to self and others"—actually flourish outside of the walls of these institutions serves only to strengthen the illusory protections which marriage and the madhouse provide against the inexorable uncertainties and vicissitudes of life. Moreover, as marriage without a marriage certificate would not be a marriage at all, so madness without a madness certificate—a commitment paper or at least a forbidding psychiatric diagnosis—would not be madness at all. These solemn ceremonial acts transform the citizen into a "psychotic patient," his protector-persecutor into a "psychiatric physician," and the relationship between them into the "treatment of schizophrenic (or other) psychosis." This is why I believe that just as there could be no meaningful protection of wives against husbands (and vice versa) so long as women were not completely free to sever the bonds of holy matrimony that tied them to their partners, so there can be no meaningful protection of mental patients against institutional psychiatrists (and vice versa) so long as persons accused of mental illness are not completely free to sever the bonds of psychiatric matrimony that tie them to their partners.

Moreover, as we now recognize that the traditional conditions and roles of women as socially inadequate or impaired persons were both the cause and consequence of arranged marriage, we should also recognize that the modern conditions and roles of certain socially inadequate or impaired persons, now often called "schizophrenics," are both the cause and the consequence of arranged psychiatry: in each case, the care and control of one party by another is secured by elevating the dominant partner and debasing the submissive one, rendering the former coercive and intolerant, and the latter counter-coercive and intolerable. Arranged marriage was, of course, the characteristic marital pattern of feudal, patriarchal societies. Arranged medicine, first developed in psychiatry, is the characteristic medical pattern of modern, (nominally) egalitarian societies. In general, the more ostensibly egalitarian a society is or aspires to be, the more it has recourse to social control by means of arranged—compulsory, state-financed, and state-regulated—medical and psychiatric patterns of prescribed pairings.

In both the matrimonial and medical relationship, each party is, of course, subject to loss of control of the relationship. In the arranged marriage it was typically the wife who lost control of the relationship, became submissive or rebellious, and often ended up retaliating against her husband's domination by tormenting him. Occasionally the husband lost control to the wife or her family, and it was then he who reacted with inadequacy, "mental illness," or suicidal aggression.

Similarly, in the arranged psychiatric matrimony of institutional psychiatry, it was typically the patient who lost control of the relationship, became submissive or rebellious, and often ended up retaliating against the psychiatrist's domination by tormenting him with his incurability. Occasionally the psychiatrist lost control to the patient or his family, and it was then he who reacted with confusion, "mental illness," or suicidal aggression.

Modern medical arrangements of the socialist, communist, or welfare type—with the relationship between patient and physician being arranged for them, both losing the power to control it, the patient usually more than the doctor—follow the pattern of the pairings characteristic of arranged marriage and arranged psychiatry. Insofar as the patient does not pay for the care he receives, he loses a large measure of control over it; insofar as the physician is not paid by the patient, he, too, loses control over the relationship, usually to whoever pays him. Thus, whereas in the past wives had been controlled by their husbands and husbands by the institution of marriage, today patients are controlled by their physicians, and physicians by the institution of medicine.

It seems best to view all of these changes—and especially the exchange of arranged marriage for arranged medicine—as manifestations of the profound social-economic metamorphoses of modern societies. The clan and the family are disappearing as significant institutions of social control. They are replaced by an old institution in a new form: medicine, traditionally an institution for curing disease, has become an institution for controlling deviance.

Finally, and perhaps most importantly, the matrimonial model of the madness network helps us to account for, and to stay clear of, both the "original" mythologies and the compensatory countermythologies characteristic of human pairings based on patterns of domination-submission. Regardless of whether these pairings are between men and women, masters and slaves, or mad-doctors and madmen, in each case we find the same sort of justificatory imagery of the superiority of the oppressor, and the same sort of counterimagery of the superiority of the oppressed.[56]

SCHIZOPHRENIA

In short, although schizophrenia is not a disease, the term *schizophrenia* is not necessarily meaningless: like the term *marriage*, it usually refers to a complex and highly variable—from time to time, class to class, and culture to culture—set of acts on the part of "patients," "psychiatrists," and the audience encouraging, discouraging, and witnessing their performance. We can, if we wish, rededicate ourselves to an effort to understand these acts and relationships and to alter them in ways we deem desirable. But we cannot do this so long as we remain psychiatrists. As husbands and wives create each other through the existential bond between them, so madmen and mad-doctors also create each other. Herein lies the medical tragedy, and the moral challenge, of psychosis and psychiatry.

Chapter 5

Madness, Misbehavior, and Mental Illness: A Review and a Restatement

IN THE PREVIOUS CHAPTERS I retraced the development of modern psychiatry; reconstructed the origin and nature of anti-psychiatry; reviewed the present status of the concept of schizophrenia; and recommended the socially prescribed pairing of husband and wife in matrimony as a fresh paradigm for the pairing of psychiatrist and psychotic in psychiatry. In this chapter I want to return to the origins of psychiatry, reconsider its "progress" to the present, and recast my thesis in a broader historical and philosophical perspective.

The first step in the history of psychiatry was the building of madhouses or insane asylums.[1] This created two symmetrical populations: one group, the larger one, comprising the inmates of insane asylums; the other, the smaller one, comprising the managers or superintendents of such asylums and the keepers who worked under them. The conduct of both groups created a demand for description and explanation.

Thus was generated the second step, which consisted of the keepers' identification and classification of both their inmates' and their own conduct. These acts of naming and ordering—resulting in the categorization of the inmates as dangerous and deranged, and of the keepers as kind and helpful—provided a scientific rationalization for the fictions of the madhouse-keepers and a legal justification for the fetters in which they confined their victims.[2]

The third step—ushering in the era of so-called "moral treatment" in psychiatry, and covering approximately the first half of the nineteenth century—consisted of the increasingly explicit recognition, on the one hand, that madmen were categorized as mad because of their misbehavior, rather than because they were ill; and of the recognition, on the other hand, that alienists were expected to teach madmen to behave properly, rather than to cure them of any actual disease.[3] However, this imagery and policy were inconsistent with the facts that, although the mad-doctors acted more as wardens than as physicians, they were, in the main, medical doctors; and that although the madmen and madwomen were deprived of liberty, they were, in fact, innocent of any legally adjudicated wrongdoing. The pressures generated by these inconsistencies, together with the rapid development of scientific medicine, especially pathology, around the turn of the nineteenth century, led to the next development in psychiatry.

The next, or fourth, step thus consisted of the medicalizing—that is, psychopathologizing—of the misbehavior of the inmates of insane asylums, and of the corresponding medicalizing—that is, psychotherapizing—of the behavior of the persons charged with their "care." This led to the psychopathologizing of many kinds of behaviors exhibited by persons both inside and outside of asylums (for example, the "neuroses" and "perversions"), and to the psychotherapizing of many kinds of behaviors exhibited by physicians both inside and outside of mental institutions (for example, "hypnosis" and "electrotherapy"). With the soil so well fertilized, a luxuriant growth of new mental diseases and treatments was soon ready for harvesting. The first crop yielded numerous new species of psychopathological syndromes and classes, such as dementia praecox, manic-depressive psychosis, and schizophrenia, associated with the names of Kraepelin and Bleuler. The next crop, in rotation as it were, yielded numerous new species of psychotherapeutic methods, such as hypnosis, psychoanalysis, and insulin shock, associated with the names of Janet, Freud, and Sakel.[4]

The next, or fifth step, beginning roughly around World War I, was marked by the literalization of what had theretofore been understood to be the somewhat metaphorical vocabulary of psychiatry. Henceforth, mental patients were considered to be sick because they had diagnoses like "schizophrenia" and their confinement was considered to be justified because it took place in buildings called "hospitals." This post-World War I era of psychiatry was characterized by the stubborn insistence of psychiatrists on seeing what is not there—namely, the organic lesions, or somatic basis, of mental diseases; and on not seeing what is there—namely, the unjust and unjustifiable incarceration of innocent persons in insane asylums. The conceptualization of "schizophrenia" as a (mental) disease thus became the sacred symbol of institutional psychiatry, and the true nature of closed psychiatric institutions became the sacred taboo of "scientific" psychiatry. Henceforth, physicians and psychiatrists, as well as lawyers and laymen, would avert their eyes from the world and fix their gaze upon heaven: the more obvious it was that schizophrenics were imprisoned, the less attention psychiatrists, and others, would pay to their imprisonment; and the more difficult it became to discover the brain lesions that cause schizophrenia, the more earnestly psychiatrists, and others, would search for them.

The sixth step, begun in the 1930s and becoming the dominant fashion after World War II, consisted of the development of so-called organic therapies—first for schizophrenia, then for other "psychoses," and before long, for all mental diseases. Since after a century of search psychiatrists could still not demonstrate the characteristic histopathology, much less the organic etiology, of schizophrenia, they now set out to "prove" that it is a disease by subjecting schizophrenics to various medical and surgical procedures called "treatments."

The development of modern psychiatry has thus not only differed from, but has been antithetical to, that of modern medicine. With the sole exception of the segregation of lepers (which occurred long before the birth of modern medicine), there has never been—in medicine and surgery—any kind of systematic involuntary institutionalizing of patients; nor has there been a systematic proliferation of disease names created independently of their anatomical, biochemical, microbiological, or physiological correlates. For example, until relatively recent times, physicians spoke of "venereal diseases" collectively; genuine classification of these diseases occurred only after discoveries in microbiology provided the necessary tools for it. Operation of the same principle is apparent in the identification and classification of all bodily diseases: that is, macroscopic pathological changes in organs, microscopic changes in tissues or cells, microbial invasions, and so on, are observed first; the precise naming of diseases comes next. This sequence has been systematically reversed and corrupted in psychiatry: the precise, or rather pseudoprecise, naming of alleged diseases came first; the existence of morphological pathology was postulated but never produced.

Hence the ceaseless manufacture of disease names in psychiatry, together with a total lack of evidence that any of them —from agoraphobia to schizophrenia—are caused by demonstrable brain lesions on the model of paresis.[5] It is the greatest scientific scandal of our scientific age.*

* This scandal has grown to such vast proportions that it now invades almost every nook and cranny of our daily lives. As I was writing, and then revising, this book, the American Orthopsychiatric and Psychiatric Associations furnished, through their ceaseless meddling in everybody else's business, the following example of it.

At the Fifty-second Annual Meeting of the American Orthopsychiatric Association, held in March 1975, the association's Committee on Minority Group Children declared that "Racism is the number one public health problem," and that "Racism is probably the only contagious mental disease."[6] The American Psychiatric Association did not protest against this expansion of the psychiatric nomenclature.

With the rapid pace of change in our world today, it did not take long for this piece of vicious psychiatric rhetoric to boomerang and

There is, in short, no such thing as schizophrenia. Schizophrenia is not a disease, but only the name of an alleged disease. Although there is no schizophrenia, there are, of course, countless individuals who are called "schizophrenic." Many (though by no means all) of these persons often behave and speak in ways that differ from the behavior and speech of many (though by no means all) other people in their environment. These differences in behavior and speech may, moreover, be gravely disturbing either to the so-called schizophrenic person, or to those around him, or to all concerned.

What has all this to do with medicine, or with a psychiatry that is ostensibly a medical specialty? The answer is: nothing. The articulation of diverse aspirations and the resolution of the conflicts which they generate belong in the domains of ethics and politics, rhetoric and law, aggression and defense, violence and war. Like medicine, psychiatry may, of course, contribute to the efforts of warring parties. But unlike medicine, that is

---

hit American psychiatrists, especially the Jews among them, right between the eyes. In the fall of 1975 the United Nations passed a resolution declaring that Zionism is a form of racism. This made Zionism —according to the United Nations, whose activities have until this time enjoyed the unqualified support of the American Psychiatric Association—a "contagious mental illness"! In December 1975 the Board of Trustees of the American Psychiatric Association duly adopted another "official position," this time on the United Nations' definition of racism.[7] Still refusing to see, or at least acknowledge, that the content of the term "racism," like that of "mental illness," depends on who has the power to fill that semantic bag with rhetorical hot air, the board instead denounced anti-Semitism. The irony of these developments is heightened by the fact that on February 19, 1974, the board had *unanimously* supported the United Nations in its "Decade of Action to Combat Racism and Racial Discrimination." However, the board's vote on the United Nations' resolution on Zionism was *not unanimous:* three members voted against it. Does this mean that the Board of Trustees of the American Psychiatric Association has three members who actually believe that Zionism is a "contagious mental illness"? Or that it is a form of "racism"? Or that it is both?

all psychiatry can do. In other words, as it is a mistake to confuse chemical warfare with medical science, so it is a mistake to confuse psychiatry with medicine.

Because schizophrenia is the sacred symbol, and its diagnosis is the sacred ceremonial, of traditional Kraepelinian-Bleulerian psychiatry, the ethical and epistemological premises on which this concept rests could be neither articulated nor challenged—unless, that is, the challenger was willing to risk psychiatric ostracism and to relinquish his role as a psychiatrist. It is hardly surprising, then, that psychiatrists leave these sacred aspects of schizophrenia alone. Modern society and its accredited sciences provide neither incentive nor rewards for those who might be inclined to assume a truly critical posture toward psychiatry.

There is only one major figure in modern psychiatry who has challenged the fundamental assumptions of psychiatry, and, although his scrutiny of them remained remarkably restrained, he soon left psychiatry for philosophy. I refer, of course, to Karl Jaspers (1883–1969), who, in his *General Psychopathology* —first published in 1913, and reissued in a seventh edition in 1946—offered the following far-reaching comments:

> In physical illness we so resemble the animals that experiments on the latter can be used to reach an understanding of vital bodily function in humans, though the application may be neither simple nor direct. But the concept of human psychic illness introduces a completely new dimension. Here the incompleteness and vulnerability of human beings and their freedom and infinite possibilities are themselves a cause of illness. In contrast with animals, man lacks an inborn, perfected pattern of adaptation. He has to acquire a way of life as he goes along.[8]

Although in his book, which has remained a psychiatric classic in Germany, Jaspers writes as a "phenomenological psychopathologist," his reservations about his own endeavors break through in a few phrases—hidden among thousands of others within its 900 pages—as, for example, in the following: "Our own age is characterized by the fact that psychiatrists are now performing in a secular fashion what earlier was performed on the grounds of faith." [9] Jaspers, however, fails to take the next step and state that, if this is so, the citizen of a modern—secular and free—society deserves to have as much protection by the state from coercion by psychiatrists as he does from coercion by priests. But Jaspers did record the reality of psychiatric practice as he saw it then, and as anyone who cares to look can see it now:

> Rational treatment is not really an attainable goal as regards the large majority of mental patients in the strict sense. There can only be protection of the patient and of society through hospital admission. . . . Admission to hospital often takes place against the will of the patient and therefore the psychiatrist finds himself in a different relation to his patient than other doctors. He tries to make this difference as negligible as possible by deliberately emphasizing his purely medical approach to the patient, but the latter in many cases is quite convinced that he is well and resists these medical efforts.[10]

Perhaps because he saw the enormity of this scandal, that is, of the gulf that separates psychiatric pretense from plain truth; perhaps because he could neither embrace nor reject the paternalistic "protectionism" that was, and is, so integral a part of psychiatry; perhaps for personal reasons (he was in frail health as a young man, though he lived to a ripe old age);

or perhaps for all these reasons, Jaspers quit psychiatry when he was in his thirties.[11]

Since psychiatric diagnoses, especially on involuntary subjects, are human acts that take place in a complex context of conflicting interests, it is necessary now to list, in a systematic way, the ethical, legal, and political premises that underlie traditional European psychiatry, American institutional psychiatry, and psychiatry in general as it is now practiced throughout the world.

First, the diagnosis of schizophrenia (and also that of other psychoses and of mental illnesses generally) may be based on the "behavioral symptoms" of the alleged patient. It may be made, moreover, and maintained indefinitely—even past the postmortem examination—despite the absence of demonstrable histopathology or pathophysiology. In other words, the fact that there is no "objective" method or observation by means of which anyone can demonstrate that a particular person diagnosed as schizophrenic is not schizophrenic in no way impairs the validity of "schizophrenia" as an accepted medical (psychiatric) diagnosis.

Second, the subject—the so-called "schizophrenic patient"—has no right to reject the diagnosis, the process of being diagnosed, or the treatment ostensibly justified by the diagnosis. The very idea, in this psychiatric scheme, of the psychotic patient's "rights" is as absurd as the idea, in the scheme of slavery, of the slave's "rights."

Third, the schizophrenic patient is usually considered to be "dangerous to himself and others," in ways undefined and undefinable, but which are different from those in which other persons are, or everyone is, "dangerous to himself and others."

Fourth, the foregoing characteristics of the schizophrenic "patient"—and especially the nature of his "illness" and his "dangerousness"—psychiatrically require, and legally justify, his involuntary confinement in a mental institution.

These, then, are the essential ethical, legal, and political premises of psychiatry—that is, of traditional asylum psychiatry as well as of modern institutional psychiatry. To appreciate their significance, let us compare and contrast them with the pertinent premises of medicine—that is, of traditional, nineteenth-century medicine as well as of modern hospital medicine—which may be summarized as follows:

First, the criteria and contents of what constitute disease and treatment may be defined, variously, by any or all of the parties interested and involved in it: the patient, the patient's relatives, the doctor, the medical profession, the church, the state, and so on.

Second, personally, the physician may base the diagnosis of disease on any criterion he likes, from the patient's own suffering to the suffering he causes others. Professionally, he must abide by the criteria approved by his peers. Scientifically, he may suspect disease broadly, but must diagnose it narrowly, only when his claim is supported by objectively verifiable evidence of histopathology or pathophysiology. Similar considerations apply to the criteria of what constitutes treatment.

Third, disease and its consequences are facts, and so are treatment and its consequences. These facts inform and influence the justifications patients and physicians construct to engage in or eschew various medical interventions, and especially treatments. However, when medicine is viewed as a profession serving the ideals of a free society, neither illness nor treatment justify medical intervention; only consent between the parties concerned does.[12]

Fourth, since treatment consists of the action of one person upon another, it is always, in part at least, an ethical and political act. These moral dimensions and dilemmas of medicine may be ignored or denied—and the drama of modern therapeutics is extremely useful in diverting people from them

—but they cannot be made to disappear. They are as inexorable as the moral dimensions and dilemmas of life itself, of which, of course, they are an integral part.[13] For example, whether or not pregnancy should be regarded as a disease and abortion as a treatment are questions, the answers to which cannot be provided by medical information or investigation.

Strictly speaking, medicine can be, and must be, concerned only with the histopathological or pathophysiological manifestations and consequences of diseases and their treatments. It cannot be, and must not be, concerned with the behavioral and linguistic manifestations and consequences of personal differences.[14]

It is against this background that the premises of my own position on so-called psychiatric problems may now be articulated and viewed. I maintain that the professional person or expert is, above all else, an agent. Our first duty in formulating his role and duty is to ascertain and assert whose agent he is. This is especially important when the expert is—as he almost always is in psychiatry—a party to a conflict. In traditional medicine the physician is, typically (and ideally), the agent of his patient. In traditional psychiatry the institutional psychiatrist is, typically (and ideally), the agent of his society. These facts shape many of the phenomena we now mistakenly regard and treat as "mental illnesses." My own relevant ethical, legal, and political premises are:

First, in a free society, the relations between experts and clients must be maximally contractual and minimally coercive. Penological interventions (and certain other state-coerced measures, such as collection of taxes or drafting of soldiers) ought to be sharply distinguished from those that clients seek for their own benefit and are free to accept or reject.

Second, in such a society, psychiatric practices that "patients" seek and professionals supply, and that both wish to define as medical, would be allowed to fall into whatever class the parties concerned want to place them, whereas those practices that either party rejects would be prohibited by law. The former practices would thus be like ordinary contracts—for example, a person contracting with an architect to build him a house which his relatives or friends may or may not consider to be a home—whereas the latter practices would be like crimes—for example assault, battery, or kidnapping—and would be so punishable and punished by law.

Third, the words and deeds of both psychotic and psychiatrist should be frankly recognized for what they usually are: coercions and countercoercions—sometimes literal, sometimes metaphoric.

Thus, as psychiatrists our task in coping with the problem of schizophrenia is, ironically, similar to the so-called schizophrenic's task as patient in coping with the problem of his life: we must both recognize our literalized metaphors as metaphors. However, we can do this only by stepping outside of ourselves, by taking ourselves less seriously and others more seriously, by placing performance over pride. These are, of course, just the things that, by and large, both psychotics and psychiatrists are unable or unwilling to do.[15]

In short, madman and mad-doctor, psychotic and psychiatrist, are locked in an embrace of mutual coercion, confusion, and confirmation. Hence, it is not that schizophrenia is a problem and psychiatry the solution for it, but rather that each is a facet of a more general problem or phenomenon—namely, of the varieties of human experience and expression and their social regulation. There is no problem of schizophrenia for psychiatry to solve. But there is a problem of schizophrenia-cum-psychiatry for epistemology and ethics, for philosophy and law, for society as a group and for individuals as moral agents to confront with their intelligence and to reconcile with their conscience.

Epilogue

Schizophrenia: The Sacred Symbol

ACCORDING TO its idealized image, science is an institution for the testing, treasuring, and teaching of truths. But anyone even slightly familiar wth the history of science knows that the real behavior of real scientists—and hence of real science itself—falls far short of this fantasy.[1] Nor is this really surprising. What is surprising, to me at least, is not how far science has fallen short of its promise to treasure truth and loathe lies, but how closely it has approximated it.

This is surprising because science is, after all, a human activity; because human beings are, fundamentally, gregarious and religious; and because, as a collective enterprise, science partakes of certain institutional characteristics that seem to be indispensable for the maintenance of social cohesion and an appropriate esprit de corps to sustain it. However, these human aspects of science—which perhaps also humanize it in subtle and valuable ways—make it less scientific. Indeed, they make science not only unscientific, but positively religious (and also political, economic, and so on) in character. As a result, the dominant models or paradigms of science function, in part, as quasi-religious symbols: they help to unite the scientists who labor under their protection and guidance and who spread their wonders, and they help cast out as heretics those who reject or try to replace them. The fate of Ignaz Semmelweis, who tried, prematurely and perhaps unwisely, to destory the paradigm of vapors in medicine and to replace it with that of infectious agents, may be recalled in this connection. The fiercely hostile, persecutory reactions against him and his ideas on the part of Establishment scientists—and this instance is, of course, merely an illustration to which others could easily be added—support my contention that the leading paradigms of a science serve, among other things, as its sacred symbols.

Since science is a human endeavor carried out by persons living in actual societies, it seems to me inevitable that science —all science—should come under the domination of prevailing social institutions and values. In short, all science is bound to be, to some extent, the servant of the modern nation-state and its ideology. However, inasmuch as the state wants to use science, and inasmuch as so-called natural laws are independent of the human will, it is not in the long-range interests of the state to interfere with the basic truth-seeking aims of science. If the state refuses to use those who might help it, if indeed it persecutes them, as Hitler did in the case of Jewish mathematicians, physicists, and chemists; or if the state supports the fakeries of a scientific fraud, as Stalin did in the case of Lysenko—then the state suffers, and often suffers quickly enough to make such unwisdom either exceptional or suicidal.

None of this is true in the case of the social sciences, whose so-called laws are by no means independent of the human will and the power of the state. On the contrary, in these disciplines we deal partly with descriptions of the consequences of certain power distributions—in the family, in the hospital, in society, and so on—and partly with prescriptions, often disguised as descriptions, of how such human relations ought to be arranged and managed. Here it is very much in the interests of the state to interfere with the basic truth-seeking aims of science. In the social sciences the state can use false or fake science and make it, so to speak, work: in the East the state uses Marxism, whose "validity" is in no way impaired by the inferiority of communist agriculture or industry to capitalist; in the West the state uses institutional psychiatry, whose "validity" is in no way impaired by its inability to diagnose, treat, or cure mental disease.

Moreover, even in the natural sciences, as Kuhn has noted, a paradigm is not discarded merely because it is inconsistent with fresh observation. "Once it has achieved the status of a paradigm," he writes, "a scientific theory is declared invalid only if an alternate candidate is available to take its place. . . . The decision to reject one paradigm is always simultaneously the decision to accept another." [2]

These facts about the nature of science decisively support the view—indeed, make any other view seem quite untenable—that science, too, is partly a "religious" affair. "The King is dead, long live the King," people used to say when they were ruled by monarchs. "God is dead, long live Marx, Freud, Hitler, Stalin, and Mao," people say when they think of themselves as having outgrown religion. Scientists, even qua scientists, are subject, or so I would like to suggest, to the operation of this principle: they can relinquish one paradigm only if they can put another one in its place. And such a change has a "religious" character, as Kuhn himself tacitly acknowledges: "The transfer of allegiance from paradigm to paradigm is a conversion experience [*sic*] that cannot be forced." [3] If all this is so in physics and chemistry, it is much more so in psychology and the social sciences—which are, in large part, fake sciences or pseudoreligions. This is not to say that the character of paradigms, in psychiatry just as in physics, is not informed or influenced by facts. The paresis paradigm of schizophrenia was informed by the facts of neurosyphilis. And when this paradigm will be replaced by another, it will, I am confident, be informed by the facts of psychiatric slavery. [4]

In short, I would conclude, first, that there can be no such thing as a true social science; second, that the symbolic-religious function of paradigms is much greater in the social sciences than in the natural sciences. Accordingly, schizophrenia will remain the central problem of psychiatry so long as society supports the sorts of interventions that are now defined as therapeutic for it and are imposed on persons diagnosed as schizophrenic; it will cease to be a problem when society withdraws its support from these interventions and the institutions that now promote and profit from them.

Appendices
References
Index

Appendices

References

Index

Appendix I

THE VIEW OF MENTAL ILLNESS
AS BRAIN DISEASE: A CHRONOLOGY

c. 1650–1750   Madhouses are established, first throughout Europe, then throughout the rest of the civilized world.[1]

c. 1750–1850   The trade in lunacy becomes a flourishing business; it is conducted in public and private madhouses by physicians, clergymen, and laymen alike.[2]

1841   The (British) Association of Medical Officers of Asylums and Hospitals for the Insane, the first "psychiatric" organization in the English-speaking world, is founded. It begins publishing its journal, called the *Asylum Journal,* in 1853.[3]

1844   The Association of Medical Superintendents of American Institutions for the Insane is founded. Its first official resolution is: "Resolved, that it is the unanimous sense of this convention that the attempt to abandon entirely the use of all means of personal restraint is not sanctioned by the true interests of the insane." [4] In 1921 this organization becomes the American Psychiatric Association.

c. 1800–1900   Madness (lunacy, insanity) is increasingly claimed by the professionals, and increasingly accepted by the public, to be a "disease" and "degeneration" of the brain, probably caused by masturbation.[5]

1838   Jean-Etienne Dominique Esquirol (1772–1840) drafts a new law on the insane and establishes forensic psychiatry as a legitimate medicolegal enterprise. "At the beginning of the continuous development of psychiatry," according to Karl Jaspers, "stands the outstanding personality of Esquirol. . . . [He proclaimed that] an insane asylum is a therapeutic instrument in the hands of an able physician, and our most powerful weapon against mental illness." [6]

1845   Wilhelm Griesinger (1817–1868) publishes his epoch-making *Pathologie und Therapie der psychischen Krankheiten (Pathology and Therapy of Mental Diseases)*, staking out psychiatry as a medical specialty. According to Kurt Kolle, "Scientific psychiatry did not exist until the middle of the 19th century. . . . The recognition that mentally disturbed people are sick people . . . made slow progress only after the close of the 18th century. This change of opinion and the subsequent incorporation of psychiatry into medicine was brought about by a book, published in 1845, by the German psychiatrist Griesinger. He made the significant statement . . . [that]: 'Mental diseases are diseases of the brain.' As a result of Griesinger's postulate, psychiatry became associated with natural science. Brain pathology became an important basis of psychiatry." [7]

1869   Karl Ludwig Kahlbaum (1828–1899) describes a certain pattern of behavior in mental hospital inmates, calls it "catatonia," and attributes it to excessive masturbation.[8] Catatonia and hebephrenia become, with Kraepelin, two forms of dementia praecox; and with Bleuler, two forms of schizophrenia.

1880   Jean-Martin Charcot (1825–1893) wins the recognition of the medical profession for hypnosis as a legitimate form of medical treatment in psychiatry.[9] He thus paves the way for the acceptance of the psychoneuroses as legitimate medical diseases, and of psychotherapy and psychoanalysis as legitimate medical treatments.

1884   Johann Ludwig Wilhelm Thudicum (1829–1901), pioneer neurochemist, proclaims the principle that is to become the model for the psychiatric concept of the "endogenous psychoses" as opposed to the "exogenous psychoses," that is, those caused by the ingestion of intoxicating substances or trauma to the brain: "Research on the chemistry of disease to be successful must be methodical and sustained.

It can be carried on by physicians only, requires the support of the State, and the fostering interest of the professional and intellectual classes. . . . Phosphatides are the centre, life, and chemical soul of all bioplasm whatsoever, that of plants as well as animals. . . . Many kinds of headache are probably due to intracranially brewed chemical poisons, or to poisons carried from the body to the brain by the blood, whether fermented in the body, or like alcohol, morphia, and fusel oil, formed out of the body. . . . Many forms of insanity are unquestionably the external manifestations of the effects upon the brainsubstance of poisons fermented within the body, just as the mental aberrations accompanying chronic alcoholic intoxication are the accumulated effects of a relatively simple poison fermented out of the body. These poisons we shall, I have no doubt, be able to isolate after we know the normal chemistry to its uttermost detail. And then will come in their turn the crowning discoveries to which all our efforts must ultimately be directed, namely, the discoveries of the antidotes to the poisons, and the fermenting causes and processes which produce them." [10]

c. 1890–1910   Paresis displaces masturbation as the paradigmatic cause of madness.

1893–1895   Joseph Breuer (1842–1925) and Sigmund Freud (1856–1939) rehabilitate hysteria as a "phychoneurosis," by defining imitating illness as itself an illness.[11]

1898   Emil Kraepelin (1855–1926) reinvents and introduces the term *dementia praecox* into psychiatry. (The term had been used in French psychiatry as early as 1860.) He regards dementia praecox as an "endogenous illness—that is, one not caused by external causes. It was assumed to be caused by some organic brain changes. Kraepelin was later inclined to the view that dementia praecox was of metabolic origin." [12]

1900   Freud publishes *The Interpretation of Dreams,* transforming dreams, the traditional province of the poets, into medical problems. He succeeds in securing medical recognition for a type of conversation, called "psychoanalysis," as a legitimate form of psychiatric treatment in certain "cases of mental illness." [13]

1904   Alois Alzheimer (1864–1915) publishes the first account of the histopathological changes characteristic of general paralysis of the insane or general paresis.

1904   In his textbook, *Psychiatrie,* Emil Kraepelin asserts that "syphilitic infection is an essential for the later appearance of paresis." [14]

1905   Fritz Schaudinn (1871–1906) demonstrates the Treponema pallidum (Spirochaeta pallida) in the primary lesions of syphilis and identifies it as the causative organism of syphilis.

1906   August von Wassermann (1866–1925) develops the first immunologic test for the diagnosis of syphilis.

1909   Paul Ehrlich (1854–1915) develops Salvarsan, the first of the arsphenamines, for the treatment of syphilis; arsphenamines remain the treatment of this disease until they are displaced by penicillin in 1943.

1910   Freud publishes his account of the psychopathology of Leonardo da Vinci.[15]

1911   Eugen Bleuler (1857–1930) renames and expands "dementia praecox," thus inventing "schizophrenia." [16]

1913   Hideyo Noguchi (1876–1928) and Joseph W. Moore (1879–1957) demonstrate the presence of Treponema pallidum in the tissues of the central nervous system of patients with paresis and tabes.

1917   Julius von Wagner-Jauregg (1857–1940) inoculates paretics with tertian malaria and demonstrates the therapeutic value of fever for the treatment of this disease; he receives the Nobel Prize for it in 1927.

1917   Emil Kraepelin rearticulates the primacy of the paradigm of paresis for progress in psychiatry: "The nature of most mental diseases is now obscured. But no one will deny that further research will uncover new facts in so young a science as ours; in this respect the diseases produced by syphilis are an object lesson. It is logical to assume that we shall succeed in uncovering the causes of many other types of insanity that can be prevented—perhaps even cured—though at present we have not the slightest clue. . . ." [17]

1919   Elmer E. Southard (1876–1920) proclaims the evangelical faith and missionary calling of the psychiatric crusaders: "May we not rejoice that we [psychiatrists] . . . are to be equipped by training and experience better, perhaps, than any other men to see through the apparent terrors of anarchism, of violence, of destructiveness, of paranoia—whether these tendencies are showing in capitalists or in labor leaders, in universities or in tenements, in Congress or under deserted culverts. . . . Psychiatrists must carry their analytic powers, their ingrained optimism and their tried strength of purpose not merely into the narrow circle of frank disease, but, like Seguin of old, into education; like William James, into the sphere of morals; like Isaac Ray, into jurisprudence; and above all, into economics and industry. I salute the coming years as high years for psychiatrists." [18]

This call for world conquest by psychiatry—that is, for the medicalization, psychiatrization, and therapization of every human activity—has since been reechoed by countless leading psychiatrists the world over.

Appendix II

PSYCHIATRY AND ANTI-PSYCHIATRY: THE SUPERIOR VIRTUES OF THE OPPRESSOR AND THE OPPRESSED

My suggestion that we regard the sane and the insane on the one hand, and psychiatrists and anti-psychiatrists on the other, as adversaries, each claiming superiority for himself and inferiority for his opponent, invites putting these images in the broader perspective of other superior-inferior relationships and their characteristic mythologies. I have remarked on this theme elsewhere, in connection with my analysis of the relationship between institutional psychiatrist and institutionalized mental patient and its similarities with the relationship between inquisitor and heretic.[1] Here I want to extend this sort of analysis to the relationship between psychiatrist and anti-psychiatrist, with particular emphasis on the moral character of their respective claims.

In one of his brilliant, early essays Bertrand Russell has furnished a framework into which this controversy fits perfectly. "One of the persistent delusions of mankind," Russell suggests, "is that some sections of the human race are morally better or worse than others. This belief has many different forms, none of which has any rational basis."[2] After remarking on how this human predilection finds its most obvious outlets in the chauvinisms of sex, nationality, and class, Russell notes that some people prefer to admire and aggrandize groups to which they do not belong—from which, indeed, they are excluded:

> A rather curious form of this admiration for groups to which the admirer does not belong is the belief in the superior virtue of the oppressed: subject nations, the poor, women, and children. The eighteenth century, while conquering America from the Indians, reducing the peasantry to the condition of pauper laborers, and introducing the cruelties of early industrialism, loved to sentimentalize about the "noble savage" and the "simple annals of the poor." . . . Liberals still continue to idealize the rural poor, while intellectual Socialists and Communists did the same for the urban proletariat.[3]

Russell suggests that there is something in the nature of the power relations between those who dominate and those who are dominated, and in the nature of human nature, which, together, generate these compensatory images of the superiority of the inferior. One of the most typical of these was, and remains, the mythology of feminine superiority, about whose Victorian form Russell offers this observation: "The belief in their [women's] 'spiritual' superiority was part and parcel of the determination to keep them inferior economically and politically." [4]

Insofar as the anti-psychiatrists maintain that the insane are superior to the sane—which is one of their most important doctrinal tenets—they seem to me to begin where the female superiorists have left off. They merely substitute for the "superior virtue" of oppressed women the "superior sanity" of oppressed schizophrenics. This particular game of the anti-psychiatrists seems to me to be both crude and contemptible, for the result of the idealization of the "authenticity" of insanity, of the romanticization of the "breakthrough" of psychosis, can be only one of two things, both of which I oppose.

On the one hand, the mythology of the superiority of the psychotic, like that of the superiority of women, may be part of the psychiatrist's determination to dominate him, not crassly as a lunatic, but covertly as a lost tourist. Or it may be a genuine effort to replace the special powers and privileges of the psychiatrist with those of the psychotic, in the tradition of the Christian program of replacing "the first" with "the last," or the communist program of replacing the rule of the capitalists with the "dictatorship of the proletariat."

Looking at the countless pairings of oppressors and oppressed, one must ask oneself: Why would anyone believe in the myths of the superiority of either? It is possible to answer this question with some useful generalizations. In the main, people will believe in the superiority of the oppressor when the oppressor occupies a favored position—for example, as a man or psychiatrist; or when they seek the oppressor's protection—for example, as a child or hospitalized mental patient; or when they wish to play a complementary role—for example, as wife or psychotic. On the other hand, people will believe in the superiority of the oppressed—for example, women and psychotics—mainly when they feel guilty toward them. Support for the countermythology is thus much less secure than for the mythology; this difference accounts for the much greater stability of the former as compared to the latter. Russell's remarks in this connection are perhaps more relevant today to the situation in psychiatry and anti-psychiatry than to any other aspect of the power politics of the human tragicomedy:

> As it appears from the various instances that we have considered, the stage in which superior virtue is attributed to the oppressed is transient and unstable. It begins only when the oppressors come to

have a bad conscience, and this only happens when their power is no longer secure. The idealizing of the victim is useful for a time: if virtue is the greatest of goods, and if subjection makes people virtuous, it is kind to refuse them power, since it would destroy their virtue. . . . It was a fine self-sacrifice on the part of men to relieve women of the dirty work of politics. . . . But sooner or later the oppressed class will argue that its superior virtue is a reason in favor of its having power, and the oppressors will find their own weapons turned against them. When at last power has been equalized, it becomes apparent to everybody that all the talk about superior virtue was nonsense, and that it was quite unnecessary as a basis for the claim to equality.[5]

It is precisely this sort of commonsense, middle of the road position to which I have tried to cleave in my approach to that still relatively unexplored dimension of domination and subjection—the relations between mad-doctors and madmen, psychiatrists and psychotics, schizophrenia experts and schizophrenics. Thus, I have tried to destroy the mythology of the medical superiority of psychiatry and psychoanalysis over legal and religious principles and practices of social control, and of the moral superiority of psychiatrists and psychoanalysts over people generally and so-called mentally ill persons in particular. At the same time, I have tried to avoid idealizing insanity as supersanity, and mythologizing the madman as a person of superior artistic, moral, or psychological gifts, virtues, or powers.

In sum, it seems to me that if the ideas I have set forth here, and elsewhere, are valid, and if they gain wider adherence, then psychiatry, as we now know it, would gradually disappear. Specifically, involuntary psychiatry, like involuntary servitude, would be abolished, and the various types of voluntary psychiatric interventions would be reclassified and reassessed, each according to its true nature and actual characteristics. Some of these practices might then reemerge as medical interventions, perhaps vis-à-vis persons who do not suffer from demonstrable bodily illnesses—a practice by no means limited to psychiatry. Most psychiatric practices, however, would either disappear or reappear as ethical and political interventions. These psychiatric practices, vis-à-vis voluntary clients, would then be recognized for what I believe they really are, namely, the "theories" and "techniques" of—or, better, the justifications for and the applications of—various systems of secular ethics.

References

Acknowledgments

1. See T. S. Szasz, "Some Observations on the Relationship Between Psychiatry and the Law," *A.M.A., Archives of Psychiatry and Neurology* 75 (1956): 297–315; idem, "Malingering: Diagnosis or Social Condemnation?" ibid. 76 (1956): 432–443; idem, "The Problem of Psychiatric Nosology," *American Journal of Psychiatry* 114 (1957): 405–413; idem, "Some Observations on the Use of Tranquilizing Drugs," *A.M.A., Archives of Psychiatry and Neurology* 77 (1957): 86–92; idem, "Commitment of the Mentally Ill: Treatment or Social Restraint?" *Journal of Nervous and Mental Diseases* 125 (1957): 293–307; idem, "Psychiatry, Ethics, and the Criminal Law," *Columbia Law Review* 58 (1958): 183–198; idem, "The Myth of Mental Illness," *American Psychologist* 15 (1960): 113–118; and idem, "Mental Illness as a Metaphor," *Nature* 242 (March 30, 1973): 305–307.

Chapter 1

1. A. B. Barach, *Famous American Trademarks* (Washington, D.C.: Public Affairs Press, 1971), pp. 43–44.

2. See, generally, T. S. Szasz, *The Myth of Mental Illness: Foundations of a Theory of Personal Conduct* (New York: Hoeber-Harper, 1961); rev. ed. (New York: Harper & Row, 1974).

3. Quoted in M. B. Strauss, ed., *Familiar Medical Quotations* (Boston: Little, Brown, 1968), p. 651.

4. G. Zilboorg, *A History of Medical Psychology* (New York: Norton, 1941), p. 44.

5. See, for example, S. Freud, "An Outline of Psycho-Analysis" (1938), in *The Standard Edition of the Complete Psychological Works of Sigmund Freud* (London: Hogarth, 1964), vol. 23, pp. 139–207; see also footnote, pp. 9–10.

6. See W. L. Breutsch, "Neurosyphilitic Conditions: General Paralysis, General Paresis, Dementia Paralytica, Chronic Brain Syndrome Asso-

References

ciated with Syphilitic Meningoencephalitis," in *American Handbook of Psychiatry*, ed. S. Arieti, vol. 2, pp. 1003–1020 (New York: Basic Books, 1959); p. 1005.

7. See, generally, *Encyclopaedia Britannica*, 15th ed., s.v. "Rudolf Virchow," and E. H. Ackerknecht, *Rudolf Virchow: Doctor, Statesman, Anthropologist* (Madison: University of Wisconsin Press, 1953).

8. See *Funk and Wagnall's New Standard Encyclopedia*, 6th ed., s.v. "Rudolf Virchow."

9. S. Freud, "An Autobiographical Study" (1925), in *Standard Edition*, vol. 20, pp. 1–74; p. 25.

10. Ibid.

11. S. Arieti, "Schizophrenia: The Manifest Symptomatology, The Psychodynamic and Formal Mechanisms," in *American Handbook of Psychiatry*, ed. Arieti, vol. 1, pp. 455–484; p. 456.

12. Ibid.

13. I. R. C. Batchelor, *Henderson and Gillespie's Textbook of Psychiatry*, 10th ed. (London: Oxford University Press, 1969), p. 247.

14. E. Bleuler, *Dementia Praecox or the Group of Schizophrenias* (1911), trans. Joseph Zinkin (New York: International Universities Press, 1950), p. 9.

15. Ibid., esp. pp. 147–160.

16. Ibid., p. 147.

17. Ibid., p. 148.

18. Ibid., p. 151.

19. Ibid., p. 428.

20. Ibid., p. 429.

21. Ibid.

22. In this connection see T. S. Szasz, *Heresies* (Garden City, N.Y.: Doubleday-Anchor, 1976).

23. See W. McGuire, ed., *The Freud/Jung Letters: The Correspondence between Sigmund Freud and C. G. Jung*, trans. Ralph Mannheim and R. F. C. Hull (Princeton: Princeton University Press, 1974), facing p. 207.

24. S. Freud, "The Psychopathology of Everyday Life" (1901), in *Standard Edition*, vol. 6.

25. J. Strachey, introduction, ibid., pp. xiii–xiv.

26. Freud, "Psychopathology," p. 257.

27. World Health Organization, *Report of the International Pilot Study of Schizophrenia, Vol. I: Results of the Initial Evaluation Phase* (Geneva: World Health Organization, 1973).

28. Ibid., p. 10.

29. E. Bleuler, *Autistic Undisciplined Thinking in Medicine and How to Overcome It* (1919), trans. and ed. Ernest Harms, with a preface by Manfred Bleuler (Darien, Conn.: Hafner Publishing Co., 1970), pp. 113–114.

30. Ibid., p. 182.

31. In this connection see, generally, F. A. Hayek, *The Counter-Revolution of Science: Studies on the Abuse of Reason* (1955) (New York: Free Press, 1964); and, specifically, T. S. Szasz, *The Manufacture of Madness: A Comparative Study of the Inquisition and the Mental Health Movement* (New York: Harper & Row, 1970).

32. Bleuler, *Dementia Praecox*, p. 474.

33. Ibid., pp. 474–475.

34. See, for example, R. M. Cover, *Justice Accused: Antislavery and the Judicial Process* (New Haven: Yale University Press, 1975).

35. See T. S. Szasz, "Involuntary Mental Hospitalization: A Crime Against Humanity" (1968), in *Ideology and Insanity: Essays on the Psychiatric Dehumanization of Man* (Garden City, N.Y.: Doubleday-Anchor, 1970), pp. 113–139; and idem, *Psychiatric Slavery* (New York: Free Press, 1977).

36. Bleuler, *Dementia Praecox*, p. 475.

37. Ibid.

38. Ibid.

39. Ibid., p. 488.

40. Ibid., pp. 488–489.

41. Bleuler, *Autistic Undisciplined Thinking*.

42. M. Bleuler, Preface (1969) to E. Bleuler, *Autistic Undisciplined Thinking*, pp. xiii–xix; p. xv.

43. E. Bleuler, *Autistic Undisciplined Thinking*, p. 43.

44. Ibid., pp. 43–44.

45. Ibid., p. 72.

46. Ibid., p. 109.

47. Ibid., p. 110.

48. Ibid., p. 115.

49. Ibid., p. 116.

50. M. Bleuler, Preface to *Autistic Undisciplined Thinking*, p. xvi.

51. Ibid.

52. See "Eucharist" in *Sacramentum Mundi: An Encyclopedia of Theology* (New York: Herder and Herder, 1968), vol. 2, p. 257.

53. "Transubstantiation," *Encyclopaedia Britannica*, 1973, vol. 22, p. 175.

54. See E. Watanabe, "The Past, Present, and Future of Mental Hospitals in Japan," *Journal of the National Association of Private Psychiatric Hospitals* 5 (1973): 6–8.

55. For example, see I. Veith, "The Far East: Reflections on the Psychological Foundations," in *World History of Psychiatry*, ed. J. Howells, pp. 662–703 (New York: Brunner/Mazel, 1975), pp. 690–691.

56. K. Menninger, *The Vital Balance: The Life Process in Mental Health and Illness* (New York: Viking, 1963).

57. Freud, "Psycho-Analytic Notes on an Autobiographical Account of a Case of Paranoia (Dementia Paranoides)" (1911), in *Standard Edition*, vol. 12, pp. 1–82.

References

58. Freud to Jung, May 6, 1908, in *Freud/Jung Letters,* ed. McGuire, p. 147.

59. Freud to Jung, June 30, 1908, ibid., p. 162.

60. Jung to Freud, October 21, 1908, ibid., p. 174.

61. See R. Graves, *The Greek Myths* (Middlesex: Penguin, 1955), vol. 2, pp. 354–356.

62. E. Kraepelin, *One Hundred Years of Psychiatry* (1917), trans. Wade Baskin (New York: Philosophical Library, 1962), pp. 151–152.

63. World Health Organization, *Report,* p. 17.

Chapter 2

1. T. S. Szasz, *The Myth of Mental Illness: Foundations of a Theory of Personal Conduct* (New York: Hoeber-Harper, 1961); rev. ed. (New York: Harper & Row, 1974).

2. B. Beyer, *Die Bestrebungen zur Reform des Irrenwesen* (Halle am Saale: Carl Marhold Verlagsbuchhandlung, 1912), p. 180.

3. R. D. Laing, *The Divided Self: An Existential Study in Sanity and Madness* (1960) (Baltimore: Penguin, 1965).

4. R. D. Laing and A. Esterson, *Sanity, Madness, and the Family: Vol. I, Families of Schizophrenics* (New York: Basic Books, 1964).

5. K. Minogue, *The Liberal Mind* (London: Methuen, 1963), especially pp. 6–13.

6. D. Martin, *Tracts Against the Times* (Guildford and London: Lutterworth Press, 1973), p. 66.

7. Ibid., p. 68.

8. Ibid., p. 75.

9. Ibid., p. 83.

10. Ibid., p. 87.

11. Quoted in R. I. Evans, *R. D. Laing: The Man and His Ideas* (New York: Dutton, 1976), p. 115.

12. Martin, *Tracts Against the Times,* p. 89.

13. Ibid., p. 90.

14. See, for example, R. M. Weaver, *The Ethics of Rhetoric* (Chicago: Regnery, 1953); R. L. Johanessen, R. Stickland, and R. T. Eubanks, eds., *Language Is Sermonic: Richard M. Weaver on the Nature of Rhetoric* (Baton Rouge: Louisiana State University Press, 1970); and T. S. Szasz, *Karl Kraus and the Soul-Doctors: A Pioneer Critic and His Criticism of Psychiatry and Psychoanalysis* (Baton Rouge: Louisiana State University Press, 1976).

15. L. Trilling, *Sincerity and Authenticity* (Cambridge, Mass.: Harvard University Press, 1972), p. 124.

16. Ibid., p. 125.

17. Ibid., p. 160.

18. Ibid., p. 168.

19. Ibid., p. 169.
20. See T. S. Szasz, *Heresies* (Garden City, N.Y.: Doubleday-Anchor, 1976), and idem, *Karl Kraus*.
21. Quoted in Trilling, *Sincerity and Authenticity*, p. 170.
22. D. Cooper, *The Death of the Family* (New York: Pantheon, 1970), p. 103.
23. Ibid., p. 33.
24. Ibid., pp. 61, 63.
25. D. Cooper, Introduction to *The Dialectics of Liberation*, ed. D. Cooper, pp. 7–11 (Middlesex: Penguin, 1968), p. 10.
26. Cooper, *Death of the Family*, p. 78.
27. Quoted in Evans, *R. D. Laing*, p. 108.
28. Cooper, *Death of the Family*, pp. 111–112.
29. Ibid., pp. 127, 138.
30. Philadelphia Association, *Philadelphia Association Report, 1965–1969* (London: Philadelphia Association, n.d.), dedication page.
31. Ibid., p. 2.
32. Ibid., p. 3.
33. Ibid., p. 7.
34. Ibid., p. 11.
35. See W. F. May, "Code, Covenant, Contract, or Philanthropy," *The Hastings Center Report* 5 (1975): 29–38; p. 31.
36. See, generally, L. von Mises, *Human Action: A Treatise on Economics* (New Haven: Yale University Press, 1949).
37. *The Human Context* 5 (1973): inside cover.
38. M. Barnes and J. Berke, *Mary Barnes: Two Accounts of a Journey Through Madness* (London: MacGibbon and Kee, 1971; New York: Harcourt Brace Jovanovich, 1972).
39. Advertisement for the American edition, *New York Times Book Review*, April 9, 1972, p. 31.
40. Ibid.
41. Barnes and Berke, *Mary Barnes*, p. 6.
42. Ibid., p. 150.
43. Ibid., p. 157.
44. R. D. Laing, *The Politics of Experience and the Bird of Paradise* (Harmondsworth: Penguin, 1967), p. 11.
45. Quoted in Evans, *R. D. Laing*, p. 115.
46. Ibid.
47. Ibid., p. 112.
48. Ibid., p. 12.
49. Ibid.
50. Laing, *Politics of Experience*, p. 156.
51. Ibid., p. 107.
52. Ibid.
53. Ibid., p. 110.
54. Barnes and Berke, *Mary Barnes*, p. 160.

References

55. Martin, *Tracts Against the Times,* p. 83.

56. Ibid., (London ed.), dust jacket.

57. See, for example, C. Fenichel, *The Psychoanalytic Theory of Neurosis* (New York: Norton, 1945), p. 283.

58. E. Fromm, *Escape from Freedom* (New York: Rinehart, 1941).

59. Cooper, *Death of the Family,* p. 93.

60. D. Cooper, *Psychiatry and Anti-Psychiatry* (London: Tavistock, 1967), p. 45.

61. J. R. Searle, "How to Derive 'Ought' from 'Is,' " in *The Is-Ought Question: A Collection of Papers on the Central Problem of Moral Philosophy,* ed. W. D. Hudson, pp. 120–134 (London: Macmillan, 1969), p. 132.

62. Ibid.

63. See T. S. Szasz, *The Manufacture of Madness: A Comparative Study of the Inquisition and the Mental Health Movement* (New York: Harper & Row, 1970), esp. pp. 260–292.

Chapter 3

1. L. C. Kolb, *Noyes' Modern Clinical Psychiatry,* 8th ed. (Philadelphia: Saunders, 1973), p. 349.

2. S. Arieti, ed., *The World Biennial of Psychiatry and Psychotherapy: Vol. I, 1971* (New York: Basic Books, 1970).

3. A. V. Snezhnevsky, "Symptom, Syndrome, Disease: A Clinical Method in Psychiatry," in ibid., pp. 151–164; concerning Snezhnevsky see, for example, H. V. Dicks, "Soviet Abuses (Two Letters to the Editor)," *Psychiatric News* 11 (February 6, 1976): 2.

4. A. Kiev, ed., *Psychiatry in the Communist World* (New York: Science House, 1968).

5. F. J. Kallmann, *The Genetics of Schizophrenia: A Study of Heredity and Reproduction in the Families of 1,087 Schizophrenics* (New York: J. J. Augustin, 1938), pp. 27–28.

6. E. Kringlen, "New Studies on the Genetics of Schizophrenia," in *World Biennial,* ed. Arieti, pp. 476–501; p. 476.

7. See L. G. Stevenson, *Nobel Prize Winners in Medicine and Physiology, 1901–1950* (New York: Henry Schuman, 1953), p. 264.

8. E. Moniz, "How I Came to Perform Prefrontal Leucotomy" (1948), in *The Age of Madness: The History of Involuntary Mental Hospitalization Presented in Selected Texts,* ed. T. S. Szasz, pp. 157–160 (Garden City, N.Y.: Doubleday-Anchor, 1973), p. 158.

9. In this connection see T. S. Szasz, *Heresies* (Garden City, N.Y.: Doubleday-Anchor, 1976), esp. pp. 3–11.

10. Moniz, "How I Came to Perform," p. 159.

11. "What's New," *Current Prescribing,* March 1975, p. 9.

12. R. E. Kendell, "The Concept of Disease and Its Implications for Psychiatry," *British Journal of Psychiatry* 127 (1975): 305–315; see also idem, *The Role of Diagnosis in Psychiatry* (Oxford: Blackwell Scientific Publications, 1975).

13. See R. J. Stoller et al., "A Symposium: Should Homosexuality Be in the APA Nomenclature?" *American Journal of Psychiatry* 130 (1973): 1207–1216; R. Lyons, "Psychiatrists, in a Shift, Declare Homosexuality No Mental Illness," *New York Times,* December 16, 1973, pp. 1, 25; "Deleting Homosexuality As Illness: A Psychiatric Change in Values," *Roche Report: Frontiers of Psychiatry* 4 (February 1, 1974): 1–2.

14. Kendell, "Concept of Disease," p. 314.

15. Ibid.

16. A. H. Urmer, "Implications of California's New Mental Health Law," *American Journal of Psychiatry* 132 (1975): 251–254.

17. Ibid., p. 253.

18. The Committee on Nomenclature and Statistics of the American Psychiatric Association, *DSM-II: Diagnostic and Statistical Manual of Mental Disorders,* 2nd ed. (Washington, D.C.: American Psychiatric Association, 1968).

19. See Kolb, *Noyes' Modern Clinical Psychiatry,* 8th ed., p. 312; and "Schizophrenia and Alcoholism Head Listing of Inpatient Ills," *Roche Report: Frontiers of Psychiatry* 5 (April 1, 1975): 2.

20. See, for example, T. S. Szasz, *Law, Liberty, and Psychiatry: An Inquiry into the Social Uses of Mental Health Practices* (New York: Macmillan, 1963), and idem, *The Manufacture of Madness: A Comparative Study of the Inquisition and the Mental Health Movement* (New York: Harper & Row, 1970).

21. R. Marlowe, *The Modesto Relocation Project: The Social Psychological Consequences of Relocation of Geriatric State Hospital Patients,* Bureau of Research Projects, 1–60 (MOD) (Sacramento: California Department of Mental Hygiene, 1972).

22. M. Greenblatt and E. Glazier, "The Phasing Out of Mental Hospitals in the United States," *American Journal of Psychiatry* 132 (1975): 1135–1140; p. 1137.

23. See, for example, L. Srole et al., *Mental Health in the Metropolis: The Midtown Manhattan Study* (New York: McGraw-Hill, 1962), and K. Menninger et al., *The Vital Balance: The Life Process in Mental Health and Illness* (New York: Viking, 1963).

24. See T. S. Szasz, "The Right to Health," *Georgetown Law Journal* 57 (1969): 734–751; and idem, *Psychiatric Slavery* (New York: Free Press, 1977).

25. "Oppressive Psychiatry," *Bethlem and Maudsley Gazette* (London), Autumn 1975, pp. 9–12.

26. Ibid., p. 9.

27. Ibid.

28. Ibid., p. 10.

29. Ibid.

30. D. Herbstein, "One Jew's Journey," *New Statesman* (London), January 24, 1975, p. 106.

31. Ibid.

32. Ibid.

33. Kendell, *Role of Diagnosis,* p. 80.

34. Quoted in H. M. Schmeck, Jr., "National Genetics Study Urged as Step to New Era in Medicine," *New York Times,* June 16, 1970, p. 1.

35. J. Huxley et al., "Schizophrenia as a Genetic Morphism," *Nature,* 204 (October 17, 1964): 220–221; p. 220.

36. L. L. Heston, "The Genetics of Schizophrenia and Schizoid Disease," *Science* 167 (January 16, 1970): 249–256; pp. 249, 255.

37. E. Cumming, "Epidemiology: Some Unresolved Problems," *American Journal of Psychiatry* 126 (1970): 121–122; p. 122.

38. "Two Minds on Schizophrenia," *New Scientist,* December 10, 1970, p. 424.

39. See "Schizophrenia: Nationality Key to Diagnosis; American MDs Make Diagnosis Twice as Frequently as British," *Clinical Psychiatry News* 2 (November 1974): 1; see also Kendell, *Role of Diagnosis.*

40. Quoted in "Schizophrenia Not Indigenous to West," *Clinical Psychiatry News* 2 (November 1974): 1.

41. Quoted in "Once a Schizophrenic Always a Schizophrenic in the Soviet Union," ibid.

42. Ibid., pp. 1, 22.

43. Kallmann, *Genetics of Schizophrenia,* pp. 102–103.

44. See Szasz, *Heresies.*

45. See Szasz, *Law, Liberty, and Psychiatry,* and idem, *Psychiatric Justice* (New York: Macmillan, 1965).

46. D. Hawkins and L. Pauling, eds., *Orthomolecular Psychiatry: Treatment of Schizophrenia* (San Francisco: W. H. Freeman, 1973).

47. Pauling, Preface to ibid., pp. v–ix; p. v.

48. Ibid.

49. Ibid., pp. v–vi.

50. See T. S. Szasz, *The Ethics of Psychoanalysis: The Theory and Method of Autonomous Psychotherapy,* rev. ed. (New York: Basic Books/Harper Colophon, 1974).

51. Pauling, Preface to *Orthomolecular Psychiatry,* p. vii.

52. For a carefully reasoned criticism of schizophrenia research in general, and of Pauling's contributions to it in particular, see R. Fischer, "Schizophrenia Research in Biological Perspective," in *Genetic Factors in Schizophrenia,* ed. A. R. Kaplan, pp. 74–138 (Springfield, Ill.: Charles C. Thomas, 1972).

53. A. Hoffer and H. Osmond, *What You Should Know About*

Schizophrenia (Ann Arbor, Mich.: American Schizophrenia Foundation, 1965), facing p. 1.

54. Ibid., p. 1.

55. Ibid., p. 2.

56. Ibid., p. 12.

57. Ibid.

58. G. Gerlach, "How Two Groups Aim to Help Sufferers From Schizophrenia," *National Observer,* Oct. 10, 1966; reprinted in a pamphlet by the American Schizophrenia Foundation, Box 160, Ann Arbor, Michigan 48107, n.d. Quoted from the pamphlet.

59. *The 12 Steps of S. A.* (Saskatoon, Saskatchewan, P. O. Box 913: Schizophrenics International, n.d.).

60. Editorial, "Diagnosis: A New Era," *Schizophrenia Bulletin,* no. 11, Winter 1974, pp. 18–20; pp. 18–19.

61. For some recent comments see "Megavitamins and Mental Disease," *Medical World News,* August 11, 1975, pp. 71–82, and "Megavitamins for Schizophrenia?" ibid., November 3, 1975, pp. 31–36.

62. S. Berman, "Fasting: An Old Cure for Fat, A New Treatment for Schizophrenia," *Science Digest,* 79 (1976): 27–31; p. 27.

63. Ibid.

64. Ibid., p. 28.

65. S. Arieti, "An Overview of Schizophrenia from a Predominantly Psychological Approach," *American Journal of Psychiatry* 131 (1974): 241–249; p. 248.

66. See Hammer v. Rosen, 7 A. D. 2d 216, 181 N.Y.S. 2d 805 (Sup. Ct., McNally, J., dissenting in part, 1959), pp. 805–808.

67. Ibid., p. 807.

68. Hammer v. Rosen, 7 N.Y. 2d 376, 379–380, 165 N.E. 2d 756, 757, 198 N.Y.S. 2d 65 (1960).

69. A. Parras, "The Lounge: Treatment for Chronic Schizophrenics," *Schizophrenia Bulletin,* no. 10, Fall 1974, pp. 93–96; pp. 93, 96.

70. See T. S. Szasz, "Medical Metaphorology," *American Psychologist* 30 (1975): 859–861.

71. J. G. Gunderson and L. R. Mosher, "The Cost of Schizophrenia," *American Journal of Psychiatry* 132 (1975): 901–906; p. 901.

72. Ibid., p. 902.

73. Ibid.

74. Ibid., p. 905.

75. Ibid.

76. J. K. Wing, "Psychiatry in the Soviet Union," *British Medical Journal* 1 (March 9, 1974): 433–436; p. 433.

77. Ibid., p. 435.

78. Ibid.

79. See J. Burnham, *Suicide of the West: An Essay on the Meaning and Destiny of Liberalism* (New Rochelle, N.Y.: Arlington House, 1964).

80. See especially T. S. Szasz, *The Myth of Mental Illness: Foundations of a Theory of Personal Conduct* (New York: Hoeber-Harper, 1961); rev. ed. (New York: Harper & Row, 1974); and idem, *Ideology and Insanity: Essays on the Psychiatric Dehumanization of Man* (Garden City, N.Y.: Doubleday-Anchor, 1970).

81. H. R. Huessy, "Some Historical Antecedents of Current American Mental Health Practices," *Psychiatric Annals* 4 (1974): 31–39; p. 38.

82. See T. S. Szasz, "Reflections on Medical Ethics," in T. S. Szasz, *The Theology of Medicine* (New York: Harper & Row, in preparation).

83. See Chapter 1.

84. Szasz, *Manufacture of Madness.*

Chapter 4

1. See T. S. Kuhn, *The Structure of Scientific Revolutions* (Chicago: University of Chicago Press, 1962), esp. pp. 77, 150.

2. See, generally, S. Arieti, *The Interpretation of Schizophrenia,* rev. ed. (New York: Basic Books, 1974).

3. See, generally, "Marriage," in *International Encyclopedia of the Social Sciences,* ed. D. L. Sills, vol. 10, pp. 1–23 (New York: Macmillan and Free Press, 1968).

4. *Encyclopaedia Britannica,* 14th ed., s.v. M. Rheinstein, "Marriage," p. 927.

5. Ibid., p. 928.

6. Ibid., s.v. J. D. Landis, "Marriage and Family Organization," p. 928.

7. Ibid.

8. Deut. 24:1.

9. St. Matthew 5:31–32.

10. I Corinthians 7:1–2.

11. Ibid., 7:9.

12. Ibid., 7:4; see also "Vatican Statements on Sexual Ethics," *New York Times,* January 16, 1976, p. 11.

13. I Corinthians 7:6–9.

14. Ibid., 7:11.

15. J. Dominian, *Marital Breakdown* (Harmondsworth:Penguin, 1969), p. 155.

16. Shakespeare, *Hamlet,* act 3, sc. 1.

17. F. J. Kallman, *The Genetics of Schizophrenia: A Study of Heredity and Reproduction in the Families of 1,087 Schizophrenics* (New York: J. J. Augustin, 1938), p. 48.

18. Ibid.

19. "Miss Nelson, 103, Dies; Confined for a Century," *New York Times,* Feb. 2, 1975, p. 49.

20. See T. S. Szasz, ed., *The Age of Madness: A History of Involun-*

tary Mental Hospitalization Presented in Selected Texts (Garden City, N.Y.: Doubleday-Anchor, 1973).

21. D. Defoe, "Demand for Public Control of Madhouses" (1728), in ibid., pp. 7–8.

22. J. Milton, "The Second Defense of the People of England" (1654), in J. Milton, *Areopagitica and Of Education, With Autobiographical Passages from Other Prose Works,* ed. George H. Sabine, pp. 93–107 (Northbrook, Ill.: AHM Publishing Corp., 1951), p. 104.

23. See W. Ll. Parry-Jones, *The Trade in Lunacy: A Study of Private Madhouses in England in the Eighteenth and Nineteenth Centuries* (London: Routledge & Kegan Paul, 1972).

24. Quoted in A. Deutsch, *The Mentally Ill in America: A History of Their Care and Treatment from Colonial Times,* 2nd ed. (New York: Columbia University Press, 1952), p. 424.

25. J. Pearson, *Edward the Rake: An Unwholesome Biography of Edward VII* (New York: Harcourt Brace Jovanovich, 1975), pp. 68–69.

26. E. Bleuler, *Dementia Praecox or the Group of Schizophrenias* (1911), trans. Joseph Zinkin (New York: International Universities Press, 1950), p. 335.

27. Ibid.

28. See E. Goffman, "The Moral Career of the Mental Patient," in E. Goffman, *Asylums: Essays on the Social Situation of Mental Patients and Other Inmates,* pp. 125–169 (Garden City, N.Y.: Doubleday-Anchor, 1961).

29. See H. Troyat, *Tolstoy* (1965), trans. Nancy Amphoux (New York: Dell, 1969).

30. L. Tolstoy, *The Kreutzer Sonata* (1889), trans. Ayler Maude, in L. Tolstoy, *The Death of Ivan Ilych and Other Stories,* pp. 157–239 (New York: Signet, 1960), p. 178.

31. Ibid., p. 192.

32. Ibid., p. 194.

33. Ibid., pp. 200–201.

34. J. Horwitz, *Natural Enemies* (New York: Holt, Rinehart and Winston, 1975), p. 2.

35. Ibid., p. 30.

36. Ibid., p. 32.

37. Ibid., p. 179.

38. Ibid., p. 202.

39. Ibid., p. 185.

40. Ibid., p. 191.

41. Y. Mishima, *Forbidden Colors* (1951), trans. Alfred H. Marks (New York: Berkley, 1974), p. 29.

42. Ibid., p. 33.

43. A. P. Chekhov, *Ward No. 6* (1892), trans. B. G. Guerney, in *Short Novels of the Masters,* ed. C. Neider, pp. 386–438 (New York: Holt, Rinehart and Winston, 1962).

44. Mishima, *Forbidden Colors,* p. 126.

45. S. O'Sullivan, "Single Life in a Double Bed," *Harper's,* November 1975, pp. 45–52; p. 50.

46. L. A. Westoff, "Two-time Winners," *New York Times Magazine,* August 10, 1975, pp. 10–15; p. 13.

47. See, for example, A. M. Freedman et al., *Modern Synopsis of Comprehensive Textbook of Psychiatry* (Baltimore: Williams & Wilkins, 1972), p. 240.

48. Westoff, "Two-time Winners," p. 15.

49. In this connection see T. S. Szasz, *The Ethics of Psychoanalysis: The Theory and Method of Autonomous Psychotherapy,* rev. ed. (New York: Basic Books/Harper Colophon, 1974); and idem, *The Second Sin* (Garden City, N.Y.: Doubleday-Anchor, 1973), esp. pp. 77–124.

50. See T. S. Szasz, *The Manufacture of Madness: A Comparative Study of the Inquisition and the Mental Health Movement* (New York: Harper & Row, 1970).

51. See T. S. Szasz, *Ceremonial Chemistry: The Ritual Persecution of Drugs, Addicts, and Pushers* (Garden City, N.Y.: Doubleday, 1974).

52. Landis, "Marriage and Family Organization," p. 929.

53. See p. 37.

54. See I. Veith, "The Far East: Reflections on the Psychological Foundations," in *World History of Psychiatry,* ed. J. Howells, pp. 662–703 (New York: Brunner/Mazel, 1975), esp. pp. 690–691.

55. M. Kato, "Present Problems in Mental Hospitals," *Journal of the National Association of Private Psychiatric Hospitals* 5 (1973): 5.

56. See Chapters 2 and 3.

Chapter 5

1. See, generally, R. Hunter and I. MacAlpine, *Three Hundred Years of Psychiatry, 1535–1860* (London: Oxford University Press, 1963); G. Rosen, *Madness in Society: Chapters in the Historical Sociology of Mental Illness* (Chicago: University of Chicago Press, 1968); and M. Foucault, *Madness and Civilization: A History of Insanity in the Age of Reason,* trans. Richard Howard (New York: Pantheon, 1965).

2. See, generally, T. S. Szasz, *Ideology and Insanity: Essays on the Psychiatric Dehumanization of Man* (Garden City, N.Y.: Doubleday-Anchor, 1970), and idem, *The Age of Madness: A History of Involuntary Mental Hospitalization Presented in Selected Texts* (Garden City, N.Y.: Doubleday-Anchor, 1973).

3. See, generally, A. Deutsch, *The Mentally Ill in America; A History of Their Care and Treatment from Colonial Times,* 2nd ed. (New York: Columbia University Press, 1949), esp. pp. 88–113, and S. J. Bockoven, *Moral Treatment in American Psychiatry* (New York: Springer, 1963).

4. See, generally, G. Zilboorg, *A History of Medical Psychology*

(New York: Norton, 1941), esp. chaps. 9 and 10, and H. F. Ellenberger, *The Discovery of the Unconscious: The History and Evolution of Dynamic Psychiatry* (New York: Basic Books, 1970).

5. See, generally, T. S. Szasz, *The Myth of Mental Illness: Foundations of a Theory of Personal Conduct* (New York: Hoeber-Harper, 1961); rev. ed. (New York: Harper & Row, 1974); and idem, *The Manufacture of Madness: A Comparative Study of the Inquisition and the Mental Health Movement* (New York: Harper & Row, 1970).

6. A. Herndon, "Racism Said to Be America's Chief Mental Health Problem," *Psychiatric News,* April 16, 1975, p. 25.

7. "Trustees Protest UN Zionism Resolution, Withdraw Support," *Psychiatric News,* January 21, 1976, pp. 1, 30.

8. K. Jaspers, *General Psychopathology* (1913, 1946), 7th ed., trans. J. Hoenig and M. W. Hamilton (Chicago: University of Chicago Press, 1963), p. 8.

9. Ibid., p. 807.

10. Ibid., pp. 839–840.

11. H. Saner, *Karl Jaspers, in Selbtzeugnissen und Bilddokumenten* (Reinbeck bei Hamburg: Rohwolt, 1970); see also, K. Jaspers, "Philosophical Autobiography," in *The Philosophy of Karl Jaspers,* ed. A. P. Schilpp, pp. 3–94 (New York: Tudor, 1957).

12. T. S. Szasz, "Reflections on Medical Ethics," in T. S. Szasz, *The Theology of Medicine* (New York: Harper & Row, in preparation).

13. Ibid.

14. See Szasz, *Myth of Mental Illness.*

15. In this connection see T. S. Szasz, *The Second Sin* (Garden City, N.Y.: Doubleday, 1973), and idem, *Heresies* (Garden City, N.Y.: Doubleday-Anchor, 1976).

Epilogue

1. See, generally, T. S. Kuhn, *The Structure of Scientific Revolutions* (Chicago: University of Chicago Press, 1962).

2. Ibid., p. 77.

3. Ibid., p. 150.

4. See T. S. Szasz, *Psychiatric Slavery* (New York: Free Press, 1977).

Appendix I

1. See, for example, M. Foucault, *Madness and Civilization: A History of Insanity in the Age of Reason* (1961), trans. Richard Howard (New York: Pantheon, 1965), and T. S. Szasz, ed., *The Age of Madness: A History of Involuntary Mental Hospitalization Presented in Selected Texts* (Garden City, N.Y.: Doubleday-Anchor, 1973).

References

2. See, for example, W. Ll. Parry-Jones, *The Trade in Lunacy: A Study of Private Madhouses in England in the Eighteenth and Nineteenth Centuries* (London: Routledge & Kegan Paul, 1973).

3. Ibid., p. 89.

4. Quoted in N. Ridenour, *Mental Health in the United States: A Fifty Year History* (Cambridge: Harvard University Press, 1961), p. 76.

5. See, for example, T. S. Szasz, *The Manufacture of Madness: A Comparative Study of the Inquisition and the Mental Health Movement* (New York: Harper & Row, 1970).

6. Quoted in H. F. Ellenberger, "Psychiatry from Ancient to Modern Times," in *American Handbook of Psychiatry*, ed. S. Arieti, 2nd ed., pp. 3–27 (New York: Basic Books, 1974), p. 21.

7. K. Kolle, "Karl Jaspers as Psychopathologist," in *The Philosophy of Karl Jaspers*, ed. P. A. Schlipp, pp. 437–466 (New York: Tudor, 1957), pp. 439–440.

8. See E. H. Hare, "Masturbatory Insanity: The History of an Idea," *Journal of Mental Science* 108 (1962): 1–25; p. 21.

9. See G. Zilboorg, *A History of Medical Psychology* (New York: Norton, 1941), pp. 362–363.

10. J. L. W. Thudicum, *A Treatise on the Chemical Constitution of the Brain* (1884), with a new historical introduction by David L. Krabkin (Hamden, Conn.: Archon Books, 1962), pp. xi-xiii.

11. See J. Breuer and S. Freud, "Studies on Hysteria" (1893–1895), in *The Standard Edition of the Complete Psychological Works of Sigmund Freud* (London: Hogarth, 1955), vol. 2.

12. Zilboorg, *History of Medical Psychology*, p. 457.

13. See S. Freud, "The Interpretation of Dreams," I and II (1900), in *Standard Edition*, vols. 4 and 5.

14. Quoted in Zilboorg, *History of Medical Psychology*, p. 543.

15. S. Freud, "Leonardo da Vinci and a Memory of his Childhood" (1910), in *Standard Edition*, vol. 11, pp. 57–137.

16. See E. Bleuler, *Dementia Praecox or the Group of Schizophrenias* (1911), trans. Joseph Zinkin (New York: International Universities Press, 1950).

17. E. Kraepelin, *One Hundred Years of Psychiatry* (1917), trans. Wade Baskin (New York: Philosophical Library, 1962), pp. 151–152.

18. Quoted in K. Menninger, "The Academic Lecture: Hope," *American Journal of Psychiatry* 116 (1959): 481–491; p. 489.

Appendix II

1. T. S. Szasz, *The Manufacture of Madness: A Comparative Study of the Inquisition and the Mental Health Movement* (New York: Harper & Row, 1970), esp. pp. 260–292.

2. B. Russell, "The Superior Virtue of the Oppressed," in B. Russell, *Unpopular Essays,* pp. 58–64 (New York: Simon and Schuster, 1950), p. 58.

3. Ibid., pp. 58–59.

4. Ibid., p. 61.

5. Ibid., p. 63.

Index

Alienists, 22n
Alzheimer, Alois, 11, 210
American Journal of Psychiatry, 96, 104
American Orthopsychiatric Association, 190n
American Psychiatric Association, 94, 96, 190n, 191n, 207
American Schizophrenia Foundation, 113
Anti-psychiatry, 48–83, 212–214; asylum psychiatry and, 73–74; authenticity and, 57, 82; cant of, 57–59; freedom and, 78; literalized metaphor of schizophrenia in, 74n; Martin's criitcism of, 54–55; Marxism and, 51, 56; paradigm of, 79–80; plundered-mind image in, 79–83; "promotion ceremonies" in, 75–76; psychiatry and psychoanalysis as similar to, 52–55, 78; sanity in view of, 82; Trilling's criticism of, 56–59; *See also* Cooper, David; Laing, Ronald D.
Arieti, Silvano, 10, 11, 89, 118–119
Association of Medical Officers of Asylums and Hospitals, 207
Association of Medical Superintendents of American Institutions for the Insane, 207
Asuni, Tolani, 106
Asylums: Laingian, 62, 64, 65, 73–74; *See also* Lunatic asylums
Authenticity, anti-psychiatry and, 57, 82

Autistic Undisciplined Thinking in Medicine and How to Overcome It (Bleuler), 27–31

Barnes, Mary, 67–70, 73–77
Batchelor, I. R. C., 12
Beating of patient, as treatment for schizophrenia, 119–120
Berke, Joseph, 67–69, 74–75
Berman, Steve, 117
Beyer, Bernhard, 48n
Bichat, Xavier, 8–9
Bleuler, Eugen, 3, 8, 9, 11–17, 19–32, 35, 38, 41, 154n, 210; *Autistic Undisciplined Thinking in Medicine and How to Overcome It*, 27–31; on concept of disease, 29–30; dementia praecox or schizophrenia as defined by, 12–13; on hospitalization of schizophrenics, 22–26; on linguistic behavior, 13–15; on pressures to diagnose as sick, 21n; on suicidal drive of schizophrenics, 25, 26; on thinking disorders, 13
Bleuler, Manfred, 28, 32
Brown, Bertram S., 123
Burghölzlihospital, 32, 65, 154n

California, LPS Act in, 96–97
Cant, anti-psychiatric, 57–59